About the Author

Dr. Arun Surendran is the Strategic Director and Principal of Trinity College of Engineering Trivandrum where he pioneered faculty entrepreneurship. He holds his Masters and PhD in Aerospace Engineering from the Texas A&M University after his BTech from IIT Bombay. He was awarded the prestigious Eppright Outstanding International Student award, the highest honor given by the Texas A&M University to any international student.

Dr. Arun is the Honorary Fellow for Robotics for the Kerala Startup Mission. He is one of the founder directors of Zenletics Cybersecurity Solutions. Dr. Arun serves as the Operations Advisor to Al Adrak Construction conglomerate in the Middle East and is the Data Science Adviser for dataPowa UK.

In 2015, he coauthored his first book on entrepreneurship, The Startup Habit with Dr. K C C Nair. Stirrups, his first collection of poems, has also been published.

Praise for *The 7 Cs of* Entrepreneurship

The 7 Cs of Entrepreneurship is a must have guidebook for any aspiring start-up buff. Dr. Arun Surendran has smoothly weaved the seven types of yarn that normally make up the fabric of free entreprise essentials. The book places a special interest in faculty start-ups, the inevitable step forward in an increasingly budget restricted business of education. University researchers will therefore find this tome of entrepreneurial framework much more relevant within the context of academia than any business plan textbooks out there. The book concludes with an inspiring and important note on resilience. Check it out!

Dr. David Natarajan
Head of Research, Universiti Teknologi MARA, Malaysia

Coming with ample hands-on experience in entrepreneurship, Dr. Arun Surendran provides a wholesome step-by-step guide for startups in every phase. With his extraordinary talent for strategic thinking as well as easy-to-read phrasing, this 7Cs framework comes along peppered with a lot of best cases to inspire and realistic considerations to protect the aspiring entrepreneurs from failing. An exceptionally helpful book!

Juliane Neubueser, Founder, JNM Education, Berlin

The 7Cs of Entrepreneurship is a must read for anyone thinking of starting a business or have already started a business and thinking of what's next? The book is comprehensive and has a structured approach towards what to anticipate in the startup environment. Dr. Arun Surendran has a knack of presenting complex ideas and thoughts into comprehensible, crisp snippets which are easily adaptable to daily life.

Seenu Kurien, National Sales Head, Corporate Social Responsibility,
Times Group

A book that surpasses expectations and delivers more than it promises. An absorbing read for a lay person and a breakthrough for an aspiring entrepreneur . Lucid , easy to grasp with simplified powerful concepts it's a fund of sound business principles and dynamic execution.
This is a book to be referred to at every stage, a book that infuses confidence. Hands on , doable it's a sure shot way to great ideas and great startups!

Jaya Chandrasekhar, UPSC Coach

The 7 Cs of
ENTREPRENEURSHIP

A FRAMEWORK FOR STARTUPS

DR. ARUN SURENDRAN

Contents

Foreword

Dr Arun Surendran is a dynamic personality, with his fingers in many pies at the same time. After completing his PhD in Texas A&M University in USA, he returned to India and took over the reins of Trinity Engineering College, Trivandrum. He is unlike a typical PhD personality, full of life and always looking forward to a fresh challenge. Arun is also my colleague as a Senior Fellow with the Kerala StartUp Mission, a Kerala Government Initiative. He is an Entrepreneur in his own way and has rolled out a few ventures of his own.

Whilst he gets a "Ground Level" view of startup scene with his innumerous initiatives at the College, the "Bird's Eye View" is provided with his work with the Kerala Government. Kerala, here in India is not quite San Francisco or Israel or Singapore, with majority still preferring to be employed with a sedate lifestyle. However, he has successfully managed to infuse the zest of entrepreneurship into the students of his college and they have come up with some remarkable products. He also voluntarily spreads his knowledge amongst the entrepreneurship community here, with weekly book reading sessions as well as interactions with successful entrepreneurs.

Having worked on such a wide canvas, everyone needs to sit up and listen when Dr Arun Surendran speaks about Start Ups. He has worked his way up with the basic principles and the 7 C's are the backbone of any Start Up. The book has been written in a fluid as well as direct manner and will act a ready reckoner for all those wishing to either start something on their own or upscale or innovate.

If you feel that you have Mission in your lives and want to achieve something greater than yourselves, grab your copy of "The 7 Cs of Entrepreneurship" and dive straight in. Use every principle outlined in the book to pivot on crucial points, dodge the incoming missiles and keep moving forward. Every word in the book is anchored in reality.

Cdr RR Shibu (Retd)
Sr Fellow (Aerospace & Defence), Kerala StartUp Mission
Founder & CEO - Hatch Spaces & Haspaces IT & Hospitality
Mentor, Accelerator & StartUp Enthusiast

Acknowledgment

The engineer-turned-entrepreneur that I get to watch in-action up close and personal is Dr. Thomas Alexander, CEO of Al Adrak and Chairman of Trinity College of Engineering. Having access to such a visionary business leader can itself be life changing, not to mention the incredible impact of the caring friend-philosopher-guide position that he occupies for me, personally and professionally. I thank him for being there through the ups and downs of the last decade.

My first book on entrepreneurship was coauthored with Dr. KCC Nair who is aptly known as the Father of Business Incubation in Kerala. The time I have been fortunate to spend with him continues to be educational and encouraging. Without his support and insights, the 7 Cs system would not have evolved.

The Innovation and Entrepreneurship Development Cell at Trinity College of Engineering led by faculty Deepu Sajeev and Anand Michael has been my sandbox for putting ideas to test. Their tireless enthusiasm and the inspiring effort of our student team deserve the greatest gratitude. The Trinity family enables an environment for the flourishing of ideas on its beautiful campus thanks to all the faculty, staff and students.

Most of the book writing (typing) happened during the early hours of the morning at home. It simply would not have been possible without the selfless support of my family. Several friends, successful in various spheres of life, especially business, education and media, have been kind enough to go through the manuscript and provide invaluable feedback. The friendships remain the best open university of continuous learning for me. I thank each and every one of them. Shout out to the Young Indians, the young entrepreneurs' conclave under Confederation of Indian Industry, whose Trivandrum chapters serves up wonderful discussions Monday evenings.

Special thanks to dear friend and Kerala Startup Mission colleague, Cdr R R Shibu (retd), CEO of HatchSpaces, who spends almost all of his energy and time enhancing the Startup ecosystem in Kerala, yet promptly appraised the draft and penned the foreword.

Last but not least, to all my teachers across the world, including the business gurus, who remain my guiding lights...

Introduction

We live in exciting times! Particularly exciting for us who are or wanna be entrepreneurs, startup founders and business owners!

As of writing this in 2019, India has close to 9000 startups registered through the central government's Startup India platform. The unregistered ones and the other "new business" entities would increase the total number of new ventures many fold. This is indeed a remarkable achievement for a nation that opened up its economy only in the 90s. In the last five years, India has climbed 65 places in the Ease of Doing Business ranking of the World Bank.

India is the 3rd largest startup ecosystem in the world behind USA and China. Yet, we remain in the 77th position in the Ease of Doing Business. The number of patent applications filed in India still is only a mere 5% of the number filed by China. In 2018, India added 8 Unicorns (billion dollar valued companies) while China created 20 and the USA 25. Average time to unicorn status for startup is 5 to 7 years in India while its been reduced to 4 - 6 years in China. Clearly, we have miles to go.

Both the central and state governments of India have put in place several measures to encourage youngsters to startup. In the state of Kerala, the government, through the Kerala Startup Mission, continues to try to create a vibrant and welcoming ecosystem for entrepreneurs. Bangalore, Pune, Hyderabad and NCR regions are internationally reputed startup hubs now with world class incubators. Perhaps this is the most necessary cultural overhaul of this century.

As an engineer turned entrepreneur and educator, I have had the good fortune to witness this transformation up close and personal. At the Trinity College of Engineering Trivandrum, where I serve as the Strategic Director and Principal, we pioneered faculty entrepreneurship. Faculty setting up and running core engineering companies on campus led to a realistic environment to foster innovation and entrepreneurial mindset among students. As an honorary fellow with the Kerala Startup Mission, I could see what worked well and equally importantly, what wasn't working for the ecosystem.

While the systematic focus has been mostly on students and the ideation process, the young innovators with brilliant ideas often find themselves in uncharted waters when it comes to setting up and growing the business. Ideation and design thinking are rightly stressed at one end, while paperwork and legal formalities at the other. Business model development and market analysis get frequently lost somewhere in between.

90% of startups close down in India within 5 years of establishment. Of course, startup failure rates across the globe are high. There is an inherent failure risk for any new venture. But this risk can certainly be largely diminished by careful planning, analysis and by thinking through the business model thoroughly. The time between the idea and the market launch needs to be wisely spent in meticulous analysis of the market. The business model must be created by being brutally honest about expectations and estimates. Mere wish-lists will not bring us success!

Casually browsing through Alibaba.com or even better, paying a visit to the numerous industrial zones in China will prove beyond any doubt that we are no longer in a supply centric world. The concepts that are still taught in many business schools based on supply powered economics are no longer valid. Demand is the key. Startups must create demand. Such demand creation involves thorough understanding of the market and the client. This is the core insight on which the 7C Framework that is introduced in this book, is grounded.

The 7 C Framework provides a pathway to build your startup through realistic, tangible and essential steps. Each C step namely Curation, Client, Concept, Consulting, Creation, Customisation and Competing, is sufficiently detailed in the chapters that follow. They are absolutely crucial in establishing a healthy new business. On top of that, they serve to minimize the risk and uncertainty that characterises a startup activity.

The introductory chapter sets the context for the 7 C framework. Sort of a framework for the framework! We discuss the basic elements involved in the startup journey. If you are toying with the idea of entrepreneurship, you will find the thinking tools to properly orient yourself.

Chapter one details the fundamental act of curation. Entrepreneurs are curious. They are curators of ideas, knowledge, practices. They are always on the lookout for opportunities, concepts, innovations, people, connections and possibilities. Living in our information age, the required skill is choosing wisely where to pay attention. The whole world is literally at our fingertips through the smartphone. Curation is the cure for the information overdose.

The necessary and sufficient condition for a business to exist is the paying customer. We discuss this element in the second chapter titled Client. Studying the market and profiling the client impacts everything from the viability of the business idea to its growth potential. We introduce the systematic way of doing this.

From the curated idea and identified market, we move to the concept. With professional services available for practically all the aspects of running a business, it is the business concept that sets apart any startup. Though it sounds theoretical, concept is the core engine that powers the entire enterprise. Once the entrepreneur has nailed the concept, rest of the process becomes much easier. Developing the concept is time consuming and iterative. It involves deep thinking, reflection, long discussions and facing unpleasant facts and uncomfortable figures. But it is an investment that must be made.

Consulting, the fourth C, feeds the business with new energy. It is important for refining the concept, righting the errors, figuring out overlooked aspects and incorporating unconsidered potentials. But we must choose the consultants and their importance wisely. It is different from networking. Entrepreneurs need to develop a keen ear for the useful suggestions. Consulting with mentors will bring a mix of courage and caution. How it is filtered usefully into the growth formula for the business is up to us. Curation skills, developed in the first stage, will help us here. Consulting is the stage where co-founders and the core team are finalised.

The fifth C in the 7 C framework is the creation. It is the creation of the product or service prototype that defines the startup. Simultaneously it is the process of creation of the startup itself as a legal entity. It is the conversion of the dream of the entrepreneur, through the core team, into reality.

In the penultimate C, we go back to the customer. The prototype will undergo numerous iterations of customisation. It will be fine tuned based on valid feedback and suggestions. This process will ensure that there is sufficient to substantial demand when the product meets the market.

The final C urges the startup to embrace competition. If competition can be envisioned as a game instead of war, it will spur productive growth for the company. Continuous curated market study and regular scanning of new technology are elements of competitiveness. It is a game that must be played with humility and a perpetually learning mindset.

Legendary entrepreneur Richard Branson's Virgin group has nearly 400 companies under its wings.The concluding chapter recaps the idea that almost all entrepreneurs are serial entrepreneurs. Starting up is a habit. It is a mindset and attitude that spurs the entrepreneurs to create new ventures. We will habitually curate the available information to discover potential businesses and keep on creating them for demanding markets.

There is an entire universe of wonderful books that an entrepreneur can learn from. Plenty of books are available detailing any subtopic of interest within this vast field. This book is meant to be a framework creation guide; a quick reference tool that can provide both new ideas and a structure for thinking. It is by no means exhaustive. Entrepreneurs and startup founders lead busy lives. The 7 Cs is meant as a fast read and repeat reference work.

Wishing you a wonderful startup journey!

1

Getting Started

Bill Aulet, the managing director of the Martin Trust Centre of MIT Entrepreneurship, in his inspiring book on Disciplined Entrepreneurship based on the course he teaches, gives a very clear formula for the connection between innovation and invention. MIT is one square mile area of university campus that has spawned over 30,000 startups. Currently, MIT students and alumni create close to 900 new businesses every year. The total economic value is well over 2 trillion dollars. Clearly, the campus is doing some things right about entrepreneurship.

MIT's Ed Roberts, the founder chair of the Martin Trust Centre and Professor of MIT Sloan School of business for Managing Technology had defined that Innovation as Commercialization added to Invention. So putting it mathematically, it is an addition operation:

Innovation = Invention + Commercialisation.

But from primary school mathematics we know that setting either of the right hand side values to zero can lead to trouble with the above formula. If there zero commercialization, then from the above formula, the invention becomes equal to innovation. Similarly, if there is zero invention, then mere commercialization would have to be counted as innovation. Bill Aulet, solves this dilemma by invoking multiplication instead of addition. He defines Innovation as a product of both Invention and Commercialization.

Innovation = Invention X Commercialization

With the multiplication operation, if there is either invention or commercialization is absent, then innovation is deemed zero. Commercialization element becomes integral.

When we focus too much on ideation and invention under the banner of innovation, we certainly miss out on this crucial aspect of commercialisation. Having said that, we must also draw the distinction between an innovator and an entrepreneur. As long as the core idea behind a new startup is stressed, it appears imperative that the entrepreneur has to be a technology inventor or innovator to qualify as an entrepreneur. Nothing could be farther from the truth. The most spectacular example to drive the point home is Steve Jobs.

Steve Jobs had no background of technical education. His strengths were the superb sense of aesthetics and incredible marketing skills. He had a knack for working with tech wizards and leading them to create mind blowing gadgets. And yes, he was an incredibly tough manager too. We will discuss more about him and the devices he brought to market in the chapter on curation. Similarly, there are numerous examples of successful business creators who had no background in the fields that they shined.

Quite often innovation and entrepreneurship are mentioned in the same breath leading to the belief in overlap of these two. In the engineering colleges in Kerala, we can Innovation & Entrepreneurship Development Centers (IEDCs) bringing both under the same banner. How valid is the implied relationship? An entrepreneur is the creator of an enterprise. She assumes its risks and brings together a team to work towards wealth creation. Technology innovators will certainly be part of the team. But in the business world, innovation is used in the broad sense. It does not restrict to technical innovation. We can innovate business models, marketing techniques, human resource practices, logistics and so on. Pretty much any aspect of business can be innovated.

The entrepreneur need not always create an innovation driven enterprise. In fact, most of the world's new businesses are small and medium enterprises that either replicate or toggle with tried and tested models in new markets. Only a few dozen companies are created out of patented inventions in even the most fertile of startup environments in the world. China files around 25,000 patents each year. Bulk of them are minor tweaks to existing technologies filed by big firms. But even the brand new patents are not all going to be successful in the market.

Small and Medium Enterprises and even Micro Enterprises will benefit from thinking through the 7 C Framework introduced in this book towards their launch. Even a replicated service needs thorough study of the new market it is catering to. It must customise its service continuously to remain competitive.

Granted that any business certainly begins with an idea. But too much stress on the ideation part leads to misunderstanding of what it takes to build a successful business. We will realize that as we go through the 7 C steps introduced in this book. In addition, there is also the danger of getting too attached to an idea if we have spent too much time polishing and glorifying it without putting it out to test in the real world. Ideation is stressed by startup promotion government agencies simply because it is easy to "teach and evaluate." It resonates with our education system. Plenty of studies have clearly shown success within the education system does not correlate with success in the real world, especially the business world. It is even more so when it comes to entrepreneurship. Education system teaches and evaluates our predictive and causal reasoning. But as the 2001 study by University of Virginia Professor Dr. Saras Sarasvathy points out, entrepreneurship demands effectual reasoning i.e. the ability to work more fluidly and effectively with the available resources.

Conceiving an idea, putting it into a business plan and making a powerpoint presentation in front of a panel of judges cannot indicate real world success for the startup. This is nothing but a competition format. Businessworld competition is evidently different from an award winning competition. With such competitions, we are simply evaluating on whatever we can measure without thinking whether what we are measuring really matters.

Glorifying the business plan is an academic exercise. Of course, the entrepreneur must absolutely have a plan. But that plan undergoes continuous transformation as new information presents itself from the market and the internal research. Most importantly, that real plan will not have an exit strategy that the academia insists on. Successful businesses are products of incredible passion and obsession from the founders. They create the business because they love it and want to do it for the rest of their lives full time. They are not folks who have a well laid out plan for exit. Startups that plan to die or be swallowed up in five years time weaken the economy not strengthen it.

The other misleading factor is that ideation is taught in the context of solving real world problems. It might appear to be a constructive direction. But thinking for a while about how many of the world beating businesses originated as "problem solving" models will lay bare the trouble with this approach. Inventions can come out of the problem solving approach, but do such solutions have the potential of commercialisation?! Facebook did not come about because Mark Zuckerberg was trying to solve a problem for the student community. Successful entrepreneurs have always created markets that didn't exist.

They innovated their way into customer hearts and minds by making things more convenient and enhancing lifestyle. Products and services showed the market that existing ways were inconvenient. Till the new service appeared, we were happy with the way we were doing things. Smartphone didn't appear because we had a "problem" with mobile phone, music player and internet. Smartphones just made our lives more easy by combining the three. And then it simply exploded the advertising market.

Politicians are interested in solving the problems of the society. At least, on paper. Rightly so. But entrepreneurs are not politicians. We are not interested in the popular vote or popularity. We are looking for paying customers. Otherwise, our business model should be geared towards winning prototype grants from the government. Are such businesses really wealth creators? Of course, there is a difference between having government as your customer in the long run for your business and being dependent on the government for your core idea while starting up.

Entrepreneurs should develop the capacity to think through full solution. They should not get stuck preparing for plan presentations and grant awarding competitions. Such a focus will prevent developing the complete realistic business model and growth plan. Winning a business plan competition is a world apart from creating a business that your life depends on and makes you responsible for the jobs of your employees.

I have been fortunate to work closely with founder-directors of multimillion dollar companies. They have all had humble beginnings. A small team sitting around a single table for weeks and months before things started looking up. They have the history of slow punctuated growth spurred by unswerving dedication and care from the core team. As the business grows, the number of people who depend on it exponentially increases.

Along with wealth creation, there is this wealth sharing aspect as well. The entrepreneur will be responsible for the jobs and livelihoods of hundreds of people. It is a tremendously gratifying and humbling responsibility. Behind all the glamour and glory of being a successful entrepreneur, lies this onus of ownership. It is like riding a tiger. Those who are watching will applaud your courage and the captivating spectacle. But getting off the tiger is nearly impossible. But then who wants to?! It is our tiger that we have nourished to be stronger and bigger to ride. Still, it is forever instinctively wild, so we will never be careless or let down out guard.

2

The First C: Curation

There is no information overload, only filter failure!
Clay Shirky, author and expert on internet technologies

Our interest in entrepreneurship might have begun because of several reasons.

We may be incredibly passionate about a particular sphere of human activity. We might want to create an enterprise and leave our mark there.

We might be passionate about creating wealth and new enterprises.

We can be inspired by the stories of wildly successful entrepreneurs who conquered frontiers despite overwhelming odds. The tales of passion and dedication spurring long hours of toil can be quite motivating. Listening to these wonderful personalities inspires us into action. Youtube and Ted Talks have now made it possible to listen to the experiences directly from personalities around the world. This is one of the wonderful positive impact of internet and the social media.

It may be that we want to be our own boss because we are knowledgeable in our field and leave our mark.

We can be very good team builders.

We might have acquired good experience from our job, understood the inner workings of a corporation. May be becoming just an inconsequential cog in a large corporate wheel is not our idea of a career.

Perhaps we are confident that our good education can help us build a successful business.

Possibly, we have stumbled upon an idea that appeals to us. May be we have a patent in our name from the research undertaken. May be, we have had a business idea throughout college life and time seems ripe to take the plunge.

It could be that we come from a family of businessmen and women. We had been in awe of a close relative doing very well in business. We have dreamt to be like them.

Be it passion, knowledge, an idea or personal history, inspiration is all around us. Starting up was not an easily available choice for the youth in India even just a decade ago. Only families traditionally in business created more entrepreneurs. Others overwhelmingly sought the comfort of an apparently "secure" job to settle into. Today entrepreneurship and startup are ubiquitous buzzwords. Entrepreneurship is actively promoted by the government through Startup India movement.

We live in the 4th Industrial Revolution. We live in the "Attention Economy." The largest businesses trade on the revenue generated from garnering the attention of the masses. Kim Kardashian makes one million for each social media post. Google and Facebook create mind boggling revenues by keeping people hooked to their smartphones. They are the

Attention Merchants. As the manifesto of the "Attention Resistance Movement"
states, our attention is their money.

To cite a seemingly trivial example, which newspaper or news website should we pay attention to? Or how many should we consult? It is very easy to spend hours and even the entire day going through news sites. It will be crippling if we are seeking a solid idea to start working on. We need to understand that having so many choices is not the power, but our ability and skill to limit them and curate them is the real power.

Entrepreneur must embrace the power of saying "No" to a vast majority of extremely appealing options. In a video from 1997 that is now famous on the Youtube, Steve Jobs made explicitly clear how the ability to say no was the cornerstone of deep focus. He was talking about several of Apple's pet projects being killed when he returned to the helm. He elaborated:

"But Apple suffered for several years from lousy engineering management. And there were people that were going off in 18 different directions—doing arguably interesting things in each one of them. Good engineers. Lousy management.

And what happened was, you look at the farm that's been created, with all these different animals going in different directions, and it doesn't add up. The total is *less* than the sum of the parts. And so we had to decide: What are the fundamental directions we're going in? And what makes sense and what doesn't? And there were a bunch of things that didn't. And microcosmically they might have made sense; macrocosmically they made no sense.

...When you think about focusing, you think, well, focusing is about saying yes. No.

Focusing is about saying no."

Curating Ideas

There are close to 400 companies under Virgin Atlantic Group chaired by the legendary Richard Branson. He famously carries a notebook everywhere with him. Any time an idea occurs to him or is mentioned by anyone he meets, no matter the place or time, Branson promptly notes it down in the notebook.

As entrepreneurs, we are always on the lookout for opportunities, new markets, new product or service possibilities. Even if we have fixed our patented idea to develop the business around, we need to be open to inspiring ideas about all other aspects of business building. We need to gather as many ideas as possible from around us. Brilliant ideas may come from the strangest of the places. Snippets of conversations may give us the wings we need. The last needed dose of inspiration might be found while flipping through a magazine.

We must develop the curation habit to ensure that we have a systematic way of processing these ideas and potentials. Noting down is the first step. The second is arranging and reflecting on them. We need to put them in the context of our goals and make them useful. This is pretty much the essence of curation. We must categorize and rank the ideas at the end of the day. Only with such a careful curation, they will be converted from momentary brilliance to sustained sources of energy for the business.

Poet and dramatist, T. S. Eliot asked, "Where is the wisdom we have lost in Knowledge? Where is the knowledge we have lost in information?" Scott Page, the Leonid Hurwicz Collegiate Professor of Complex Systems, Political Science and Economics at the University of

Michigan, uses this as the starting point of his 'Wisdom Hierarchy' in his incredibly informative book, The Model Thinker. At the bottom of the hierarchy lies the raw data. Named and categorised data becomes information. Rain falling on our head is data. Monthly rainfall in our hometown is information. Information becomes knowledge only when we apply relationships and logic to it. In other words, we need to curate it. And the top most tier of Wisdom is the ability to identify and apply the relevant knowledge in a given situation. Again, that is curating the knowledge.

Thus, even after we have zeroed in on an idea that we are going to pursue, we need to curate the information floods to us in the research stage. This is the stage where we beginning curating our idea towards a business concept and model.

Curation System

The Chairman Emeritus of CISCO, John Chambers, is one of the most successful CEOs in the world. Chambers took up the CEO position in 1995 and in the two decades of his leadership took CISCO from a 70 million dollar single product company to a 47 billion dollar behemoth with 18 products and 180 acquisitions. In his book, Connecting the Dots: Lessons for Leadership in a Startup World, he puts the need for curation elegantly,

"You have to develop a capacity for filtering and evaluating the facts, the fears, the fiction and the feedback that bombard you every day."

In fact, curation is the strongest habit that the entrepreneur should continuously develop and sharpen. Being in the world of business means numerous interactions, temptations, threats and considerations flitting in and out of our attention throughout the day. Our attention is the precious commodity. Paying attention is energy consuming for the brain. That is why it is called 'paying.'

Such a drain on the brain affects our will power. Roy F Baumeister, one of the most influential psychologists of our times, describes willpower in his book "Willpower: Rediscovering Greatest Human Strength" as a kind of mind muscle. Every single decision and choice we are forced to make, taxes the muscle. Sleep and sugary foods can restore the balance. But as the day progresses, our ability to resist tempting choices considerably weakens. With this awareness, it is important for us to be systematic our exposure to choices and our process of decision making. Once we develop habits of thinking, they will become easier and easier to apply.

The earlier we become systematic about prioritising our attention, the better our decision making process would be. Whenever exposed to choices for the first time, go in with an open mind. Take the time to see the merits of each option. Be brutal about the demerits. Rank them accordingly and decide which of them makes the final cut. It might be about the newspapers we read daily, relevant blogs we choose to follow or mentors we decide to embrace for life.

It doesn't mean we never again look at new choices that arise in the sector. Brand new blogs are added by the hour. Perhaps, one newspaper we rejected in our early days evolves into much high quality. It could happen that our first couple of conversations with a perfect match mentor didn't go right. To avoid missing out on these possibilities, we should keep aside time at regular intervals to rescan the whole spectrum of choices. Such revision time is important part of the curation system that we develop. It can be a relaxing exercise too during the weekends or holidays.

Entrepreneurs have a reputation as risk takers. It often conjures up the image of reckless daredevils. Successful entrepreneurs are exactly opposite. They are humble students and evaluators of risk. They take responsibility of the risk in an enterprise so that the employees can work without risk.

According to Dr. Beau Lotto, the renowned neuroscientist, creator of the Lab of Misfits and the author of Deviate, our brains have evolved to quickly remove uncertainty. Brains are prediction systems that have the sole goal of survival. Brain hates uncertainty. If we ask the questions predicated on uncertainty, brain will latch onto the easy survival solution. One such question: Will this business work? Is a question that can be easily answered with a No by the brain so that it can go back into risk free survival mode.

But the question: How can we make this work? Is grounded on Effectual Reasoning. It calls the "Slow Brain" into play. Nobel Laureate Dan Kahnemann has superbly illustrated the two modes of operation of our brain in his best seller, "Thinking, Fast and Slow." Entrepreneurs need to have their analytical, rational, logical, long term "Slow" brain alert and active. "Fast" brain is all about instinctive, impulsive, quick fixes, loss aversion and cognitive biases. It is this "fast brain" that causes us to fall for "get rich quick schemes" and to "run with the herd."

We have all experienced the silence of the our brain if at the end of a talk, the speaker urges us to ask questions. Only a handful in the audience might stand up with not so great questions after plenty of prodding. Yet, when the Q&A is over and we walk out of the hall, we all have these brilliant questions that pop up into our brains that we wished we had asked. The part of the reason for this problem here is passive listening. If we had been continuously evaluating the points of the speaker, actively thinking through the talk, then slow brain would have had questions ready. Notebook and pen are helpful tools for the slow brain.

Our brains have not evolved for careful analysis of risk and the long term potential to thrive. These are acquired skills that the brain can become quite good at, if we train it deliberately. Having a systematic way of spending our attention will also equip us to stay calm in crisis situation. One of the most desired trait in a leader is the ability to avoid panic as upsetting or shocking information flows in. If the leadership panics, the team is bound to fall apart. The leader should be able to stay grounded and evaluate the information carefully and chart a course of action.

The Other Big C: About Curiosity

Curiosity almost always tops the list of important and defining characteristics of path breaking entrepreneurs. They have an insatiable hunger for learning about everything that comes across their way. The passion to find out more with open, incessant questioning makes them stand apart.

With access to so many informative channels in our times, it is impossible not to be curious. However, we must carefully understand that there are three types of curiosity. And the most commonly found one is not very helpful beyond a certain stage. In fact, it becomes detrimental. The three types are diversive, epistemic and empathic.

Diversive curiosity is found in all primates and several other animal species and birds that are deemed intelligent to a certain level. They are inquisitive. They like to poke around if there is something new in the environment. It is an attraction to novelty. Diversive curiosity is the driving force that helps babies learn fast. But it is also the curiosity that keeps us addicted to social media and leads to immense wastage of time online. Diversive curiosity is driven by unpredictable reward system. It has been studied and documented very well by psychologists across the world. While it might lead us to new information and delight us intermittently, this kind of curiosity does not lead to productive learning and understanding. It leads to the misunderstanding that familiarity is equal to knowledge.

Epistemic Curiosity on the other hand leads to learning and understanding. It is based on the deliberate accumulation of knowledge driven by curiosity about a particular thing. It calls for investment of time and effort. This kind of curiosity leads us from finding something interesting to developing a passion for it through sustained attention and learning. Entrepreneurs must cultivate their epistemic curiosity. It places demand on our memory and slow thinking analytical brain. But the rewards are long term and long lasting.

Education system is truly beneficial only if it can transform the diversive curiosity of children into epistemic curiosity of students. Unfortunately any exam oriented system will fail in this aspect as the only performance index is the marks scored by answering particular questions. It is an "answering ability" measurement while curiosity is improved by the questioning ability. It is not much of a surprise then that traditional academic success has very little to do with entrepreneurial success.

So the entrepreneur needs to use her inherent diversive curiosity to skim through bulk of information that comes her way. Then the switch over needs to be made to epistemic curiosity to pursue the ideas worthy of time and attention. Indisciplined use of the internet and social media will lead to costly fatigue.

Empathic Curiosity is the greatest asset in both team building and market study. It helps us connect with others. Empathic curiosity can put us in their shoes. This allows us to be much more effective and understanding team leaders. Empathic curiosity reduces the ego block that usually destroys meaningful customer feedback. To navigate our way in rapidly changing market conditions and to feel the directions ahead, it is important to honestly accept the feedback that comes to us. This requires a certain level of identification with the origin of the feedback. Empathic curiosity leads to the right kind of questioning that can build relationships based on trust.

As mentioned before, the only measure of curiosity that we have is the number of questions raised. From the sense of wonder which is the immediate reward for being curious, it is questions that help us move from diversive to the epistemic curious stage. Six and seven year olds ask hundreds of questions each day. By the time, they become teenagers, the number shrinks rapidly to sheer. It is almost impossible to elicit questions from higher education classrooms. What changes? Part of the blame is the education system that stresses on knowing the answers than asking the right questions. The standard testing practices that can be cracked by repetitive mind numbing practise is surely a culprit. There is peer pressure as well. Teens are bothered if asking questions will make them seem dumb. There is also the attitude that disinterest and indifference is more "cool".

As we get into the entrepreneurial mindset, we realize that the ability to question coupled with deliberate analysis of the answers is one of the greatest assets. Most of the jobs in today's world demand the skill of managing upwards. As long as we are able to satisfy the demands of the higher ups and provide them expected responses our job is safe. For the entrepreneur, there is no higher up. It is where the buck stops. He needs to find answers from all around, from the markets, from the mentors, from the researchers, from the customers and so on.

These answers are not going to be handed out. They are not to be found in any fixed syllabus. So when the world becomes our classroom, the kid with most questions is the smartest, not the dumbest.

We are not asking the questions to impress anyone or entertain ourselves. We ask to gain clarity and better understanding. Perfect knowledge about anything is impossible. The best we can hope for is adequate understanding that can reduce the risk of our actions.

Einstein apparently quipped that it is better to be stay silent and be thought of as an idiot than to open our mouths and remove all doubts about it! It is not true in the business world. The more pertinent information we have, the better our position to act.

Curiosity leads to questions. Questions lead to clarity and understanding. Understanding prompts our action. So we must sharpen our questioning skills. Our interactions can be fruitful with a combination of open questions and closed questions. Closed questions have definite answers that we don't know yet. They are requests for information. They need to be as specific as possible. Open questions are those that open up possibilities for new questions and thought processes. We will discuss later how setting an agenda for any meeting can help us come up with a great combination of questions. In other words, we need to curate our questions as well!

Curating the Cofounders

The solo or lone wolf entrepreneur is a myth. Most of the idolized entrepreneurs of the world have had a partner or a very strong team from very early on. But we are culturally primed to be fascinated by the stories of the lone genius inventor and innovator who changes the world.

Richard Branson compared the status of the superstar entrepreneur to that of the Formula 1 driver. The driver gets all the glory in the race but has the stupendous effort of a team that has helped him drive his best. It is impossible for any one of us to have all the qualities needed to be successful. As a team, we immediately increase our chances.

Selecting our co-founders is an act of curation. Once again we need help from our analytical skills but we must also be attuned to our emotional cues when we deal with the folks who are going to work very closely with us in an open ended adventure.

Bill T Gross, the founder of the hugely successful Idealab, has a four letter system to identify the main characteristics of the founding team of a startup. His EPAI system acknowledges the Entrepreneur who has the big vision that leads the enterprise, the Producer who executes the product and the sales, the Administrator who runs the company and the Integrator who keeps it all together especially when ego crisis hits the firm. While we shouldn't get too hung up on the EPAI system, it is important to realize that the team members must have complementary strengths that help make the whole team much much greater than the sum of its parts.

The Startup journey is long and arduous. We need as the core team, people who can share the enthusiasm and are passionate about their area of expertise. The partners must keep each other motivated.

Thus with curated curiosity, we approach the world for our business idea and founding partners. We dig into our passion, our knowledge base or our skill to pick a product or service that will change the world. Now so we think. Will it really do so? We need to find out systematically. And that process begins with the identification of the Client, our second C.

3

The Second C: Client

The second C in our 7 C framework stands for Client. 'Client' is being used here as a catchall word for several concepts that will be explained through this chapter. But fundamentally, we want to stress the fact that the most Important necessary and sufficient condition for the existence of a business is the paying client. There is no survival of the company without having a paying customer. Grants, awards, loans, incubation support etc can only prop up the business for a limited amount of time. They are to be used only for survival till we find the clients who can help us grow and scale. Unless the company finds or creates a market that will pay for its products and services, the company will inevitably fail.

Through the Curation stage, we have acquired the habit of carefully picking from among the information coming at us from all corners. We keep building our capacity to convert our diverse curiosity into a powerful weapon that can lead to insights and understanding. Through this process, sooner or later, we will come across that one idea which will convince us to pursue it for the foreseeable future. It is the idea that we deem will change the world for the better. Now, with the second C, ts the time to put it to the first test.

Here's that billion dollar question we must face: Who will 'buy' our product or service? The keyword here is buy. The question is not who will like our product. The question is not which panel of judges of ideas are impressed by our presentation in a contest. The question is not even whether the idea can influence someone to fund our project. They are not the buyers. We are looking for the group who will put down their hard earned money for our product or service.

Equally importantly we must realize that those who use our product and those who pay us may be totally different sets of people. For example, If it is a social media platform we are planning, then our users might be coming in for free, but our payment is coming from the advertisers. If it is toys that we are building, children are the users but parents are the paying customers.

So who will be our buyer? It is a simple and straightforward question. But it can and must lead to long, hard research. This is the first step in our business model. We are interested in where the money is going to come from for the sustained growth of the company all through its life.

Whether we set about on our startup journey because of passion, knowhow or a unique product, we were ourselves the important players in the game. It needs to change. As humans, we are all biased towards ourselves. By default, our mind comes up with fantastic ways to protect our egos. So it is naturally for us to believe that we have a world class service to offer. Afterall, this idea convinced us to take the plunge when the habit would have just made us go on with our lives. So it has immense power over us. We have dreamt that customers will certainly be flooding through the gates as soon as we launch. In this second stage, we need to put that biased belief into rigorous test.

If we are overly attached to the idea and believe its secrecy is very important, this process is going to be tough. The feedback we will receive from potential customers will be shaky if they are asked to go through some kind of non disclosure and our questions tiptoe within a realm of fear of giving away too much. There is nearly zero chance that our idea is so totally unique that nobody else in this highly connected world has not thought in the same direction. So getting too much attached to the idea in itself without fleshing out the details is almost always futile. Letting the idea breathe by discussing it with others, actually allows it to grow.

We need to come up with questions that can bring us meaningful information about the paying customer. Our aim is to sketch out the profile of an ideal customer. Where are they based? What is their age? What do they do for a living? Are they managers, engineers, doctors or artists? What is their income? Are they men or women or does our product appeal to both? How well educated are they? Does it matter?

We are trying to figure out the age, sex, ethnicity, location, financial standing etc of that ideal person who would be thrilled to own our product by paying for it. If we are coming up with widely different possible ideal customers across several spectrums of the society, then it is warning sign for us to slow down. It means we are overestimating the value of our product or service. Without customization, it is going to difficult to capture such a wide range of customers. Our product might indeed be very appealing. But if we think it will work across such a variety of markets, then we must hunker down for a really long series of surveys and market study.

John Chambers, the legendary Cisco CEO mentioned earlier, in his book on leadership in the startup world titled "Connecting the dots" clearly lays out how he owes his tremendous success at the helm of Cisco to his continuous sincere interaction with his customers. Each product design and each of the 180 acquisitions during his tenure, were done with fully transparent consultation with the clients. It is the root cause of his success according to him. However, he also admits that a towering once in a generation genius like Steve Jobs has the unique capability to fully design and deliver a world changing product without any interaction with the customer till delivery.

Most of the wanna be entrepreneurs idolize Steve Jobs. We must realize that Steve Jobs had the support of the world's best engineers at Apple to come up with cutting edge technology that seamlessly worked within the aesthetic design and Jobs himself was a world class salesman. He had the ability to create a cult following and die hard fans who would be mesmerised by his presentation. Our circumstances are not the same. Also keep in mind that Jobs did not have a perfect track record of all products being a success. Entrepreneurship is a high risk, high reward deal even for someone with the talent and skills of Steve Jobs.

Identifying and listening to the client is the route for almost all of us to go as John Chambers points out. As we set out our company plan rooted in our curated idea, chances are that we are ourselves in a customer mindset. But this can lead to some serious issues. Since we are fathering this product, we'll always have a soft corner for our baby. That is not good for the healthy logical planning for the market. The more attached to the idea we become, the more selective our hearing will be about the feedback. We will only hear what appeals to us and readily ignore the negative feedback. This all too human cognitive flaw is called confirmation bias. It is well researched and all of us are better of being aware of this major pitfall in our thinking.

We are the creators of the product or service. We will be first users as well. We will want our baby to be as perfect as possible. But we are not the paying client. There are numerous examples of never-ending product design cycle where the creators went on adding more features to the product without ever checking with the prospective client. In this context, John Chamber is pretty crisp in his advice, "Sell only what the client needs." He categorically states that whatever we manage to sell to a client beyond their needs is going to prove very costly to us in the long run. The relationship of trust will be shaken by such deals.

So how do we find out what the client needs? As motivational speaker Jim Rohn states, the Bible has the answer: Ask! We need to arm ourselves with the art and science of asking the right questions. In this stage of our business plan, once we have sketched out the profile of our idea customer, we need to start talking to a few who fall within that category. Of course, there will not be a perfect match, but each conversation with a potential customer will enrich our planning.

There are seven billion people in the world. We are probably going to talk to only a dozen of them at this stage. So worrying about our project or the idea leaking is unnecessary. It is an immaturity most often found among student entrepreneurship who put incredible value on secrecy. Our discussions in this stage are with potential customers, not potential entrepreneurs in search for an idea. The potential customers are already busy with their work. We are sending feelers about a product that can potentially help them. They may like it or dislike it but we can be sure that they won't be quitting their jobs to develop it in direct competition to us.

We need to pick the real world versions of our "ideal customer" carefully. With social media today, it is possible to get help from anyone anywhere in the world especially if we pose the questions correctly. Face to face meetings are the best. When that is not possible, Skype or video calls can help. Emails and exchanges over social media are the last resort because they do not give us any emotional clue which are important when we are trying to understand the client reactions and attitudes.

Judging from the enthusiasm of these potential customers, we can start toggling our idea into a more concrete form. Make no mistake, sometimes our idea might die in this stage itself. We can very well be told why we misunderstood the value of such a product or that such a product already exists in some other form.

For example, among startup circles, we frequently encounter all engineer founding teams that are developing medical devices. Born out of their compassion for the needy and the suffering, these ideas and products are rarely backed by deep and latest knowledge of medical sciences or existing medical technology. These products might be very appealing as a project to other engineers but when we actually take them to a doctor, a hospital or a patient, the situation can seriously change. It is much better to shift our direction at this stage rather than go on with the launch only to realize painfully that it's a dud. All the money and time would have been wasted. These initial conversations however can give us important information of some other gap which exists in the market.

Even if they like or dislike it, each conversation will give us vital clues about the direction we need to go. We need to take notes from such meetings and find time to go over them. In other words, Curate them! Quite often something that was casual mentioned will turn out to be a crucial aspect we had overlooked. These can be revealed only if we carefully review the meeting in our memory.

We can also get a clue about how much potential clients are willing to shell out for our future service. It is necessary information as we embark on fine tuning our concept.

The ideal customer leads us to our beachhead market. This is the small slice of the total market into which we will launch. It should be safe enough which means we must be sure that it is made up of folks closest to our ideal paying customers. May be we have a product we think all working mothers will need. That's the long term big picture. For the beachhead, we can focus on say women who work in the IT industry. And within that subsection, women in a particular group of companies or a city or a certain age group. This is the segment we will target first. Both the ideal customer profile as well as our startup constraints will play important roles in how we pick. It is our beach for landing. We don't want a risky Normandy. We seek a safe port to which later on our mother ships can anchor.

Beachhead market should bring us returns that are promising enough for the overall health and growth of the company. Identifying the beachhead market will help us tune the first version of our product quickly towards the launch. Modifications and additions can be added later when we expand into bigger market cross sections. The beachhead market should provide us a solid landing so that the financial outlook and situation will provide for such growth.

Organizing surveys to study the clientele has to be done professionally. There will be agencies available who can carry out the survey for us. But we should design the questions so that we get most actionable, meaningful information towards fortifying our business idea. Even when we are engaging on, one on one, questioning, the order of the questions and setting of the meeting matter as well.

Social media provides access easily to individuals and groups that are our prime targets. It is easy to craft searches to identify them. It is possible that our beachhead market is itself already available as a Facebook group. We have to be systematic and careful while using them for our data collection. The information has to undergo extra scrutiny. We need to guard against our own confirmation bias based on the numerical strength of such groups. A group with 1000 members who fit our description of potential customers does not mean, all of them are authentically so. Assuming that members in a free social media group are going to be paying customers is faulty. We live in an age of armchair activism. It is so easy, painless and free to sign up for a group. Actually buying a product demands more time, effort and spending real money.

Numerous industry publications, databases, magazines and journals might appear as shortcuts to provide the kind of information we seek. Suppose we would like to enter the apple production industry, there would surely be an Apple Producers Journal or The Apple Magazine that will have numerous informative articles about the industry. All the curation expertise and experience we have gathered comes in handy as we process this information. The most important caveat is that this is second hand information. Our company is our own. It is our dream, passion and mission for life. We cannot solely depend on second hand information for finalizing our plans.

Whatever the magazines or social media say, we must absolutely visit with real people in real environments relevant to our planned product. There are dime a dozen examples of ruined savings because people jumped on hearsay money making opportunities. It is very tempting to either start a venture or invest in one after listening to tales of 1000% growth in some overseas market or reading a marketing spiel about assured returns in 6 months time. Second hand information must always be consumed with a big pinch of salt. We are dedicating our lives to start our venture. We need to know ourselves.

Visiting the real environments, farms, factories, offices and marketplaces will also give us a feel for how our company is going to be physically operating as well. Sooner or later, we will have to deal with these people and places. It is quite possible that all the rosy pictures in our imagination based on our reading and listening does not match with how things actually operate on the ground. Once again, taking in information ourselves from a variety of sources will provide tremendous advantage when finalizing our business concept.

Sometime ago, one of the design teams I know had worked on developing a workstation-on-wheels for a city hospital. The design process was initiated after a conversation with the lead doctor. Till the prototype was completed, the design team never visited the hospital. In their minds, it was going to be used in an environment resembling the highly sane and scripted hospital sets seen on television shows. When they finally saw the product in action inside a messy, busy, frantic emergency trauma and critical care division of the hospital, they could immediately see dozens of changes that were absolutely essential. Had they visited the hospital at least once before getting starting with the process, result would have incorporated most of the essential features saving so much money and time. This is just the case of a single design. We are talking about gathering information about our entire dream company. We must absolutely spend time on the proverbial battlegrounds where our product must fight it out and win.

By the time, we reach this stage of real world market data collection, chances are that we would have spend weeks and months curating our idea. Naturally, a certain amount of attachment would have developed to our own dreams. This must be kept in mind so that we can look at the market study and true potential of the company honestly. The fact that we have spent some time and effort already should not lead us to whitewashing the information or selective analysis to suit our plans. As mentioned earlier, confirmation bias is our great enemy. No matter how difficult it is for us to accept the discouraging information on the ground, we must take them into account. We need to maintain the strict discipline of an open mind when we face the facts. We are much better off abandoning or completely overhauling all our plans depending on the data collected. We have to search the data looking for more negative than positive feedback. Any risk seen at this point should be accounted for and carefully dealt with. Instead of getting excited about any shared enthusiasm we receive from the surveys, the focus should be on the caution advised, warnings expressed or even apathy. These are invaluable clues towards the future health of the company.

Analysing from extreme perspectives can be a technique which can help us at this point to overcome our biases. When reflecting and reviewing on the conversation or meeting, look at it from two diverse points of view. First think why things said in the conversation are supportive towards formation of the company and success of the business. Now do a second round, but this time asking if everything said in the conversation was a warning against starting such a company. Such a lens for looking at the statements made will throw more light in unexpected possibilities which might not have been explicitly stated.

Brutally honest analysis at this stage can save us all the future heartbreak. It is a tough task, but then we certainly don't want to create a company that is dead on arrival. From the wisdom gleaned out of the information obtained based on the data collected, we can proceed to craft our business concept.

4

The Third C: Concept

We have our curated idea.

We have a clear understanding of the potential market of "ideal clients" that will make our idea into a commercially viable product/service.

Now we step onto the next C in our framework: Concept.

'Concept' captures an end to end, powerful and very clear understanding of the why, what and how of the entire business.

By end to end, we mean a complete plan of starting from the resource gathering to the finished product delivery and receipt of payment. We need to be able to visualize clearly how each of those important cogs in the business wheel are going to function. The concept we craft will make them function together seamlessly.

Concept is powerful because it becomes the core mind map for us as the creators to keep referring to quickly. The concept needs time to get refined. Eventually it will be represented or expressed in very few words and pictures. And that is important. Our business concept needs to be easily understood by anyone from an investor, a banker, an employee, a potential recruit or a customer. It is more than a tagline or a marketing catchphrase. It captures the essence of the company. Writing out a business plan and putting together a business model canvas are all standard processes that help us gather more clarity towards the final concept. In this chapter, we examine the why, what and how in some detail.

The Why?

There are plenty of entrepreneurs who are rich and famous. But none of them became entrepreneurs to be rich and famous. Becoming idolised was a fallout of their exceptional success in the world of business. With the free social media and smartphones, there are so many ways to be famous and rich today. We need not start businesses to do so. We would be grossly misled if our "why?" for creating a startup is to be personally wealthy and famous.

Our initial why for thinking about the startup either came out of our passion, knowledge or specific product/service idea. At that stage, we were curating our way into better information to flesh out the idea. Only the founding team or lone founder was involved at this stage. Thus, the "why" for doing the business had very personal origins.

In the second stage, however, we met the potential customers. We studied the market. The interaction enriched our basic reason for starting the company. With the involvement of others, in this case, people who will actually pay for what we produce so that it benefits them, our initial "why" for doing the business undergoes a transformation. Apart from setting up a startup for ourselves, we see why the product matters in the world. The company is no longer coming to life because we are great engineers or leaders, but it is coming to life because it will be the channel through which our engineering expertise and leadership skills will make lives better for our customers.

Being 21st century educated citizens of the world, we must also consider how our company will impact the society and the environment. It is imperative that our business follows an environmentally sustainable model that benefits the society at large as well. These two considerations will add to the "why" in our concept. We will think through why our company will be making not only the lives of our direct customers better, but also why it will improve lives in general and make the world a better place.

There are several advantages for thinking in such a global perspective at this stage itself. First, it will help us identify markets in other parts of the world that we might have overlooked. In fact, it could happen that our truly advantageous beachhead market is on the other side of the globe. Secondly, the global view hints towards magnitude of scaling possible for our company.

Our consideration of the greater society ensures that the business is not about exploitation of human and natural resources in one part of the world for ease of life in another. Any model that is based on such exploitation will sooner or later stumble into serious problems.

Thinking on such a scale need not be scary. It is not fantasy either. The considerations for society and environment are providing us much wider footings for the stability of the business concept as we build further and further up.

As Simon Sinek, the author of the bestseller "Start with Why?" has pointed out, why we do what we do is the innermost circle that pretty much powers the "what" and the "how" of our business? The core reason keeps up the motivation. Our inner values are the best source of strength. They form the bedroom we can rely on when things get tough and they certainly will during the life of the company frequently.

The What?

What exactly do we do as a business?

Locking down the answer to this question has several uses. It helps us have a clear, simple picture of the entire process. Such a map is equivalent to the business canvas thinking to put together the business model. What do we do puts forth the areas of priority that we as founders should always keep in mind. As the business progresses, there will be numerous distractions, frequent crisis and disturbances to the smooth functioning. During those difficult times, have a clear idea about what is it that we are doing as a business can help us be calm and focused on the things that matter in the long term.

The answer to this question also shapes the elevator pitch when we are in the funding stage and marketing stage. An elaborate explanation of what we do can then be refined into pithy taglines. Google has the wonderful motto of organizing the world's information. It is a very simple straightforward and memorable phrase for what Google does or aims to do. It points to the core value proposition of our business.

What our business does can change over time. Sometimes drastically so. Western India Products, originally a vegetable oil company, has transformed itself into one of the most valuable information technology giants in the world, WIPRO. Companies should always be evolving if they are to stay in business with the changing market conditions and rapid technology advancements. In our case, we haven't yet founded the company. So here, we are striving to define value proposition.

Consider the following questions: What are we going to do first? What is our mission? What will we do to change the world through this company after its inception?

Defining and communicating these clearly among the core team is extremely important. The first days, weeks, months and in some cases even years are the toughest in the life of a startup. Temptations will be many to go after easy pickings. From a world beating initial idea, it is easy to slip down to becoming just a local small imitation business when the cash flow gets tough or design difficulties prop up. The core mission should serve as the fountain of inspiration to gather around when the going gets tough. So it makes sense to spend quality time and effort in getting it clearly defined.

How are we going to do it?

This is not about the meticulous product design method. It is not about the prototyping detail. It is about the entire operations that keep the company alive. It is the process by which we will do what we have set out to do needs to be charted out.

The product or service is our main value proposition. We are creating the plan for how we can partner with existing companies to scale up the product/service, what activities we will maintain as the core company, what all can be outsourced, how we will market to potential customers, how we will provide customer service and how we will balance our account books to generate a sustainable profit.

Reread the questions above. Each of them needs our careful consideration. We will live a supply surplus world. It is possible to find professional bodies or companies ready to provide specialized service in almost all areas. There is no need for our company to take up doing any of such service when it can be outsourced to a trusted partner.

The best example is packaging and logistics. Very few companies today have their own product packaging units. Or consider all the big technology brands. Most have simply become research, development and design companies at their core. The manufacturing, packaging and delivery of their products are all handled by third parties.

Figuring out such competent third parties and engaging them productively and profitably is one of the major elements of an entrepreneur's success. Our main competency as a company would quite often be engaging with the market. We will focus on coming up with a suitable products and sustaining the demand for such a product.

Preparing a business canvas is an absolute must at this point. Several online resources are available to create them if we do not prefer making physical ones. There is a reason why post it notes are used to stick our ideas about the various business components onto the canvas. It is important to maintain a detachment from different value propositions and customer segments we stick to the canvas. All the things we put on the canvas can change. We should be able to easily throw away our post it notes depending on new information that comes in.

The deeper our thinking at this concept stage, the smoother our subsequent steps and the final launch. One aspect that should be kept in focus is the costing. Refining the concept can be measured in terms of how much we are able to control the upfront cost. But by no means, should this become an exercise in cheapening our product or enterprise. So the quality of our outcome should be kept as a parallel measure. We should simultaneously strive for the highest quality possible at the lowest cost for the company. With these two factors pulling from either end, our concept will become tight.

A great example to help understand the importance of the concept to create a unique company is the Tea Campaign in Germany. In the late nineties, Gunter Faltin, as an economics professor, had the time at hand to shape and sharpen his idea into a foolproof concept before launching the Tea Campaign. He found that tea available in German retail outlet came at extremely high prices, in small quantities and in a variety of flavors. He wanted to reinvent the whole way tea was marketed and consumed in Germany.

He figured that the cost was high mostly because of the middlemen. Cutting them out and importing directly from producers in India was the first step. There was no particular logic for selling tea in small quantities because it did have a longer shelf life. He decided on half kilogram or one kilogram packages instead of the hundred gram packages in vogue. Finally, instead of doing a variety of flavors, he decided to stick to a single type of tea to be delivered directly to home. Market study led him to pick the most sought after Darjeeling tea. Refining the concept further, he found that exporters from India were ready to give him two months time for payment. The shipment could reach Germany in a month ready for distribution. That meant he had one month to collect payments from the consumers and pay the producer. This allowed him to drastically diminish his upfront cost.

The other great success factor in Tea Campaign is the use of professional services for all the business components. Faltin found perfect partners to deliver professional packaging, distribution, delivery and marketing services. Basically, he simply created a great business concept and found great partners to help execute. Isn't that what entrepreneurship is all about?!

Developing the concept in depth, helped him make profit from the first month. With the involvement of professional partners, he could keep his staffing to the minimum. The core team was free to constantly improve the business model. The entrepreneur was freed to conceptualize other businesses to develop and pursue.

The business concept development is where the entrepreneur is most engaged full time. In the running of the business, the entrepreneur should have minimum involvement in the day to day activities. It is for the partners, managers and employees to run the show. The concept should help us define that. The entrepreneur should be free to have all his attention in overseeing the overall health of the company and in charting its growth. Granted, she has to frequently attend to high profile clients and address the team, but she must certainly not assign herself repetitive tasks of administration and management of the company.

We have gone through curating information, discussing with potential clients to gather real data about the market and developed a concept. Developing the concept was a thought intensive, private activity which involved only the entrepreneur and the core team. Now with this concept, we step out into the world to test its merits and discover its demerits through the consulting stage of our 7 C framework.

5

The Fourth C: Consult

In this stage of the startup journey, we take our concept to an important set of people. Just like how we vetted our curated business idea by taking to real world potential customers, now we bring the business concept that we privately developed to the group of people who can give valuable suggestions and support. These include our co founders, mentors, business consultants, potential key partners and eventual investors. By consulting, not only do we refine the concept further, but we create the inner circle of dependable people around the core group. The curation abilities we gained in stages one and two will come in handy during this stage. Let us look at the categories of people we will meet for consulting with our business concept.

Consulting with Co-founders

As mentioned before, establishing a business is very rarely a solo pursuit. Even when charismatic lone wolf founders have fully stolen the limelight, there have almost always been silent co-founders and partners who have contributed immensely to the success for the firm.

We are assuming that reading this book is a solitary pursuit, so the discussion about co founders is valid from an individual founder's stand point.

In the first C of our framework, we curated our attention and understanding of our core team. We picked individual who share our passion and vision for starting up. We carefully chose those who had the knowledge or skills that will be crucial for the success of our company. But the most important aspect we kept in mind was their ability to align with the team.

If the development of the concept was a group activity that involved the core team, then this consulting will not be necessary. However, chances are that the founding team has complimentary skills and not all of them will want to get involved in the business concept development. The following discussion on this topic is relevant in such a scenario.

If your team consists of experts in different areas and they were not involved in the development of the concept, consulting with them must be done. We must keep in mind that they would be most interested in the areas of the concept that are their domains. They can offer us fine suggestions that will help us refine those aspects in the business model. At the same time, we must also listen carefully to what they have to say about other aspects of the model. These opinions must be curated. We have to weigh them appropriately. It is impossible to please everyone. So this consulting also becomes an exercise in diplomacy.

The conversations with the core team must always be open and constructive. The team is working towards a grand common goal. But everyone has an ego. The efficiency of leadership at this stage is in managing diverse opinions. Diminishing the value of a particular suggestion or an opinion must be clearly separated from devaluing the person. Everyone is attached to their opinions. So the leader must take pains to show how a particular suggestion won't be useful to the company as a whole though it has stand alone individual merit.

Another possibility is hijacking of the model by a particularly passionate member of the team. The most vocal and energetic will obviously have an advantage in terms of time and attention given to them. This should not skew the business model. Also we must be aware of the halo effect.

Halo Effect is a cognitive bias that we need to keep in mind throughout the Consulting stage of our framework. Because of Halo Effect, we tend to give unfair amount of weight to areas where it is not deserved simply because someone is exceptionally good in one area. Just because one of the co founders is a world class engineer, we tend to attach lot of value to his opinion in marketing. It is a cognitive bias that is natural. People tend to think popular actors will make good politicians or that good looking people are more honest. Let us put the halo around someone only in particular fields where they truly outshine others. Let us be careful that the light of the halo does not spill over to other areas that they are not qualified in.

Till this stage, we could operate our business on shoestring budget. Personal savings would have been enough for us to survive. We can undertake the stages discussed so far even while holding onto another job to meet our living expenses. Before we move onto the next stage of Create, we need to discuss financial arrangements with the co-founders as well. How will ownership be distributed? What equity share can the founders expect? Will there be some kind of salary? How are personal expenses to be met as we start spending full time on the new venture? The answers to these questions will depend on the nature of our startup as well as our particular circumstances.

Consulting With Mentors

Any successful entrepreneur will have at least one mentor. Usually it is a 'Tribe of Mentors' as Tim Ferris's wonderful book is titled. These may be folks from close family, distant relatives, teachers, senior colleagues or individuals we met serendipitously.

Mentor is more than an adviser or a teacher. He or She is someone who can understand the mindset of the entrepreneur. Such an understanding is not just theoretical. They can relate to the desires and fears of the startup founder because they have traversed similar paths. We will get a whole set of consultants and advisers to give us specific help in different sectors. Such experts are useful and important in our journey. But they do not come under the glorious position of mentor that we reserve for a few.

It could very well happen that someone we met initially in the role of a teacher, expert, consultant or adviser, grows to don the mantle of a mentor. That is why curation from our part is important. We need to pick wisely. Always, choose mentors who have been doers, not simply preachers. It is their experience that we will draw up on much more than their bookish knowledge.

The mentor offers help when we don't even know that we need help. The mentor keeps us grounded. The mentor shares their experience while leaving us free to draw our own lessons. We give them the freedom to ask us why we did something and expect them to ask us why not consider something out of this world!

The mentor may not even be living close to us. They can be someone we met online. There have been cases where the mentor was never contacted for a long time. Just their life's work, their words of wisdom would be suffice to keep the entrepreneur going forward for a long time. But to be really effective, we need at least one mentor who can meet up once in a while....may be monthly, may be twice a year!

The pattern of interaction will evolve over a period of time. We just need to be careful to keep the relationship serious and purposeful. The Halo Effect can affect us here as well. In our context, these mentors are business mentors. They may be able to influence us in other walks of life, but that is not our main purpose and their main role. It is up to us to refine the relationship so that it provides the best inspiration and direction for our business.

There is no rule that mentors are for life. People move on. Our business could outgrow the mentor. In that case, we will seek and find a new team of mentors who have been in similar shoes before.The focus is always on learning from their experience and observing their behavior. But we are not trying to imitate our mentors. We do not want them to set us rules or fixed pathways. They need to give us the courage to walk our paths.

Business mentors will have their own busy lives. So we need to plan the interactions so that they are able to give us their best attention. The location and timing of meetings become as important as the content discussed because of this. It is a relationship based on trust. The conversations should have clarity. These are conversations that we will ruminate on later for more ideas and motivation.

Consulting with Consultants

Consultants are professionals and experts who can offer us help and advice for a fee. It is a structured business interaction. There are already protocols and channels for availing such services. We must pick and use the best of them. Getting opinion about the consultants from other startups and our mentors will be a good idea. Consultants are also in business.

Chances are that the marketing glitz from big name consulting companies tempt us to go to them. But we are startups. Our budget is our biggest concern. Big firms come with bigger fees. They may or may not be able to provide us the attention we need. However, they did get big because they have assembled and maintained a reputation. They will also have the ability to recruit the best talent. We need to weigh these pros and cons. Small time consultancy firms and one person models might prove attractive financially for us to engage. But we must do a thorough background check. We need the right balance of expertise and budget.

Seeking someone who has a proven track record with startups, would be a neat metric to go by. As founders we certainly won't have familiarity and much less, expertise in all aspects of business creation. This makes the consultat essential players of the startup process. Our approach should be with a long term relationship in mind. Even though we might develop our own inhouse capabilities as the company grows in various business related areas, consultants will be our best support till then. They can continue to serve as advisers later on. So we need to figure out in the early stage itself, whether we can build a trustworthy, mutually beneficial and purposeful business connect with the consultants we pick.

Care must be taken to pick each one individually. It will appear rather easy to pick a few consultants in different fields based on the recommendation of one that we already picked. Let's say we found an excellent company secretary who can set up the business as legal entity for us. He or she will surely have a legal consultant and a tax consultant to recommend. One of the advantage of choosing a consulting firm is that they come with the whole team at our disposal. But if we go after individuals and depend on their recommendations of each other, chances are that even if one of them turns into a mismatch for us, it could strain our dealings with all the rest.

The online business environment allows us to utilize consultants from any part of the world. We only need to take the effort to do a careful study, conduct the first meetups and interviews and see if there is a connect that we can build on.

Government agencies provide consultancy for free in many startup environments. Business incubators can come attached with their own consultant team. In these cases, we need to see how much field experience the consultants have. If they are salaried employees whose accountability and payment are not connected directly to the quality of service, then we need to double check their intrinsic motivation to provide us the kind of service we need and deserve.

Consulting with Key Partners

Gunter Fatlin's Tea Campaign, mentioned in the previous chapter, is a perfect example of setting up a business leveraging the strength of key partners. The entrepreneurs strength is the power of the well thought out idea that is meticulously organized into a working concept. The key partners who are experienced entities in their own areas form the moving parts of the business we create. There are several extremely good logistics companies around the world who have mastered the transport industry and operate fleets with tremendous efficiency. It will be stupid for us to think about a logistics fleet of our own from scratch instead of bringing in an existing experienced logistics company as a key partner.

With industrial estates and special economic zones in all parts of the world with their focus on low cost and high quality manufacturing, key partners for creating physical products are readily available. If we consider our business as a series of operations that lead to customer satisfaction and collection of revenue, then we can see how best to bring in partners for each operation instead of doing it ourselves. Ideally, only the core management and planning should be with us.

Often, Startup teams get bogged down by trying to do all the business administration themselves. This creates unnecessary strain and is a huge waste of time and effort. As founders, our business is to grow the business. It is not predominantly to run the business. There are professionals available for that.

Once again, our curation abilities will be needed in full force in this stage. Lets be reminded again that we live in a supply side economy. We will find all kinds of producers and suppliers for any product and service. It is up to us to pick the right fit. This demands a lot of careful research and discussions from our side. Key Partners are absolutely crucial. They must fit into the overall company culture that we have in mind. Compromising on quality for saving a bit of money at this stage will be dangerous. Naturally, we will have a huge temptation to go with the cheaper service provider in all areas that we need partnership. There might be partners offering world class service at a low cost. But it needs to be double checked. Almost always, lower cost means come corners are being cut somewhere or some of the charges will become visible only down the lane.

We need key partners who have experience working with startups. It is a different ball game compared to standard B2B operations. Startups are volatile environments that need a lot of leeway and quick adaptation to changing conditions, not just in the market, but also within themselves. Partners should have had enough experience to understand this. Secondly, they should be well established , so that the partnership adds credibility to the startup itself. Picking another startup as a key partner is a risk that we should try to avoid at this stage. For some very specialised product or service, such a partnership can be inevitable, but it will mean much more effort from our side to ensure the smooth functioning of the partnership.

Another question that can bother us at this point is the number of key partners. Should be go with more or less? If one partner can provide us with several services, should we just pick them? The answer depends on the situation. The situation is similar to how we picked our consultants. It can be logical to use a single partner to take care of a few areas in our business process. But solely depending on a couple of other companies to run our whole business is akin to putting all our eggs in one basket.

Partnerships must be kept time bound. Though we enter into the business relationship with them as if it is for the entire life of the company, the market around us is evolving too quickly. New, better players appear all the time and we must not miss out. So all the partnership contracts must undergo rigorous reconsideration at the end of agreed upon periods of time. Here again, we need to consider if our attachment to a bigger brand name can cause us some damage if we ever have to let them go.

Consulting with Potential Investors

The necessary and sufficient condition for a business to exist is profit. The startup must ultimately be a wealth creator. No matter how great the concept, if it cannot attract and generate enough money for sustainable growth, it will fail over time.

We need to run our developed business concept by the people who can put money into it. Though the word investor stands for people who would buy equity in the company, we will use the term here to apply to anyone willing to give our enterprise the money. That will include bankers and government and non governmental agencies that provide funding in the form of grants and subsidies.

While "investors" will demand that they get a share of ownership in the company, bankers and others will help us if we are ready to take on debt. We may not want to consider parting with ownership at this early stage. Sharing ownership might mean management conflicts early on. If we can convince lenders, then taking on debt in the form of loans will be the better alternative. We can consider valuing the company at a later stage and then get on with equity based funding.

The bankers are an integral part of the business. Sooner or later we will need their help either as a loan for expansion or as working capital loan. It is advisable to bring a bank on board with us at this stage. In India, there are plenty of options available among the nationalised and private sector banks. We need a banker who understands and appreciates our business concept. More than that the bank should trust the founders personally for their ability to pull off.

Newspapers daily scream about the big and small defaulters who are ruining our banking system. The non performing assets are the biggest worry of any bank. It is understandable that in such scenario bankers are very wary to support any new venture. That doesn't mean that they are against new enterprises. Big and successful enterprises are the life line for bank's performance as well. Banks need good ventures as much as the ventures need the banks.

The greatest inspiration for confidence is clarity. So before we set up the meetings with our potential bankers, we must have very clear answers about the questions they are surely going to have. Preparing for such a meeting will also help us bring a lot of clarity into our financial plan. The bank should see that we are one hundred percent dedicated to the startup's success. We should make them understand how much we value their presence for our startup. Approaching them for advice at this early stage definitely makes us look good. It is a first step that we can build on.

Approach as many banks as possible till we find the right fit. Once again, we need to be careful about confusing a personal connect with an institutional connect. Just because we hit it off very well with a certain banker doesn't mean we are going to have a smooth relationship through out. More than individuals, focus on the culture of the bank. Find out if the attitude of the banker we liked is representative of the attitude of the bank towards startups.

Through these initial meetings, we must learn as much as possible. Financial world is one of rapid change. New schemes and loans are announced almost daily. One might come our way that we didn't know about but with the potential to make us rethink more than a few parts of our growth plan.

Almost all local, state and national governments around the world have woken up to the need to create and support a vibrant ecosystem. Several agencies are in place that are meant to help startups get a foothold and grow. These are organizations and agencies that we can tap into. Many of them have systems to provide startup grants. Grants obviously are much better than loans since there is no collateral and pay back. But it also means that they are difficult to obtain. And there is always intense competition.

Establishing good relationship with such government agencies is important for our business to ensure that the paperwork that is inevitable with the establishment and running of the company proceeds smoothly. Though these organisations have the mandate to assist startups, we must understand that the people involved are very rarely those with any real startup experience. Though they might be theoretically or academically knowledgeable about business, they may not have any real world experience. This could come across as a disconnect in our interactions. Plus we must always account for the possible bureaucratic delay in getting things done.

Venture Capitalists come to mind first when we talk about investors. It is a valid doubt whether to bring them into the plan at this stage of the concept. Our concept still has several iterations to undergo before it is in the final form with which we can go for fund raising to a venture capitalist. But it would be a good idea to find a friendly VC at this stage to run the idea by him. VCs have tremendous experience judging the potential of a business idea. They are, of course, not right all the time, but we need to heed their reaction to our concept. They can also give us excellent pointers which may not have crossed our minds.

Some of the biggest and most successful businesses in the world today began with borrowed funds from family and friends. This set of close people we must definitely talk to about our concept. They have known us personally over a very long period of time. Naturally, their judgement is not going to be objective at all. However, this money comes with a lot less strings attached. We might then be tempted to treat such money without much discipline. That is something we need to guard against. We do not want the business to spoil our personal relationship. So though this money comes without many rules, we need to create and stick to our own rule that paying back those who trusted us first will always remain the top priority for the company.

The business concept becomes richer with more inputs from diverse set of people. Friends and family can give us those especially when we approach them as potential investors. When they are asked to put up their money, we must discover the hidden business spirit and intelligence of those close to us. Free advice mostly has only the zero price tag as the highest value. But when we ask advice to people as potential investors, they will be more careful about analysing our concept.

The consulting stage needs to be meticulously documented. We need to keep aside time, if possible, after every meeting to go over the points discussed. We should also do an end of the day analysis. Only by digesting the interactions and pondering over the notes taken, we can extract maximum value from the consultations.

As you might have figured, we do a in-out-in-out model with the development of the business through the 7 Cs. First, we were curating inwards, then we went out into the market and checked with other. Then we were back with ourselves, making the concept. After that we are once again stepping out to meet the world. We can look at it as breathing life into our business by drawing from the world and working within alternately.

Our concept will be much more enriched at the end of this Consulting stage. We will also be energized and ready to go. So it is time to finally create what we have planned so far.

6

The Fifth C: Create

A rmed with our meticulously developed, detailed concept that has now been vetted by a bunch of expert consultants, we are ready to create our venture and the core product or service that propels it.

Let us look at the creation stage in two distinct parts. First, the creation of the product or service and then, the creation of the business itself.

Creating the Product/Service

The create stage for the product or service goes through couple of phases in which we use all the experience we have gathered so far. First we will create a prototype. The prototype is more than a working model. Working models are impressive as research and development projects. The prototype must be fully usable as intended by the final user. It is as close as possible to the final product. Only minor design changes and adjustments to suit mass manufacturing should separate the prototype from the final product that we launch into the beachhead market.

Prototype creation is time consuming. Prototyping is expensive. This is the stage where we pump in money without any immediate return. So there is a natural tendency to cut corners or opt for the cheapest option when it comes to picking the components. This must be avoided at all cost. Ensure that the prototype uses the best components with no compromise to quality.

Physical product prototyping will need us seeking out the latest manufacturing techniques. Manufacturing technology is fast evolving across the globe. Granted, we might be restricted to how much of it is available locally, but when it comes to components or parts option, we can tap into the world market if we can get the items quick enough. Idling the team simply to wait for something to arrive from somewhere is pointless and risky. So as the team leader, we need to spend serious thought about the scheduling of the prototyping process.

We might need to use facilities and equipment that is on lease or rented. Manufacturing hubs, fabrication labs, maker villages etc can be tapped into at this stage. But we must account for unexpected delays and always have a backup plan while approaching outside agencies. We have to absolutely take their help at this stage. But time is money as well.

In the case of engineering product design, renting the well equipped labs of engineering colleges can also be considered. They will provide a low cost option and usually come with good technicians who can support. A typical engineering college will have all the labs for the core engineering branches. They can be used for manufacturing as well as testing. Good colleges will have licensed analysis software packages as well. At Trinity College of Engineering in Trivandrum, where I serve as Strategic Director, industrial product prototyping is frequently undertaken not only from startups but also established companies that are looking to keep the expenses in check.

The creation stage is also the first in which we might be hiring employees or taking the help of freelancers. It is better not to commit to providing people full time jobs at this stage. A tempting option is to use student interns. But there is a limit to the quality of output that inexperienced minds can bring to the table no matter how enthusiastic they are. We need to weigh the pros and cons about each step of the prototyping stage before putting our money and faith into it. It is a connected process that needs timely action for different sets of folks.

We have already developed the profile of an ideal customer based on our market research and consulting. The design process has to be kept centered around such an ideal user. Engineers and designers are usually carried away by the latest available technology. They are biased by the niche areas of their expertise and specialisation. It is up to us to make sure that such biases are kept in check during the design and prototyping. The product or service is meant for the user. We might have to check in with a few potential users for clarifications at this stage. Such questionnaires should be created with clarity. Care should be taken that additional information available does not upset the entire design process. Be very specific about the external input that is sought and received. Design and prototyping should strictly be an internal process.

If it is a software or service that we are creating and not a physical product, then the create stage is when most of the coding happens. For a service provider startup, we need to bring in the key partners required to pull off the service. Such services should be in a soft launch mode at this stage. When it comes to software, we need to be extra careful about the licenses that are required. And that bring us to the discussion on establishing the company itself.

Let's take a moment to think about the prototype itself. We created an innovation, whether it be product or service, to perform a particular set of functions. What separates our product is how it performs these functions compared to the existing or non-existing alternatives. Here's an easy mnemonic to keep in mind the main characteristics the prototype must have: BEES!

The prototype should be able to perform the intended tasks Beautifully, Efficiently, Easily and Sustainably. Functionality is definitely the most important focus area. The prototype should do what it is meant to do. No doubt about that!

Additionally, we should prioritise the aesthetics. The "look and feel" really matter to the customer. We cannot hope to land business using a product that looks like a high school student project with hanging wires, chopped edges and shoe box casing. The prototype must execute the task efficiently.

Efficiency in terms of energy, time and money. That is what the innovation is all about. Compared to how something is done today, we are creating a better way. It should be efficient for the user as well as for us, the producers.

The prototype must be easy to use. Nobody wants something that comes with a huge manual and cognitive demands. We live in a world of "straight out of the box" and "plug and play" products. From our perspective, it must be easy to produce and easy to manage.

The product or service should also be sustainable. It should be environmentally responsible even when mass produced, be within regulatory frameworks of the industry and ideally, leave the world a better place because of its existence, in all senses.

Creating the Company

The company is a business entity with an identity and life of its own. We are its creators. But it is a legal entity more than the cofounders. Every country and states within the country have established systems for formation of companies. In India, there are multiple options for the legal businesses ranging from one Man Company to private limited company. The cost of setting up each may vary. We must study the government websites from the relevant departments to get a fairly good idea. There are plenty of professionals and companies that can help us set up. Curate the choices available and pick someone with whom we can work in the long term rather than basing the decision on cost factor alone.

While forming the firm, the "ease of doing business" in the location we have chosen becomes an important factor. When thinking about where to set up the company, we need to consider our long term growth plans as well. It might be easy to set up a small operation anywhere, but what are our prospects when we begin to scale. Can the company grow as fast as we wish it to if it were to stay in this city? Will it be better to have operations shifted to another country later? If so, do we still retain the original offices? These questions may appear irrelevant at this point, but they are not. These questions help us understand our own attitude towards expansion, growth and globalization.

Creation is the stage in which we can take help from the numerous technology business incubators and coworking spaces around the world. Even a small state like Kerala has close to two dozen incubators. Many of them are attached to different research centers or government agencies specialising in particular sectors. We can choose the incubator depending on its sector focus or its reputation for stellar support.

Sometimes trying out a brand new business incubator in the private sector might be the best option for our company.

Using the ecosystem of a business incubator will help us in several ways during this crucial step. Incubators provide support in all the required areas at an affordable rate. Since startups are their clients, they have the incentive to keep up with the latest in regulatory framework and legal requirements for startups. Well run incubators depend on the success of their incubated startups for furthering their business. So access to mentors, funding schemes and venture capitalists etc are facilitated by the incubator management team.

With such a large number and variety of incubators available, once again the curation responsibility is ours. The founding team should visit, take the tour and spend adequate time at all the incubators analysing them before taking the decision. We must have discussions with not only the incubator's marketing and management team but also the companies that are currently working there and the companies that graduated out of that incubator space successfully.

Incubator ecosystem also brings together like minded teams and potential future clients. In the case of coworking spaces where established companies also take space for the sake of convenient operation, this becomes more important. Our interaction with the employees of those business could lead to more ideas and potential sales. Being housed in a flourishing ecosystem helps us grow with more energy and better direction.

The common worry about intellectual property protection that leads some startups to set up shop separately and secretly is unnecessary. No business can grow in isolation. Afterall, our clients and markets are out there in the world. While the R&D team might work for some time in secret, sooner or later, we have to expose our creation to the world for invaluable feedback. Fear of idea being stolen is unfounded. Besides, when it comes to worthwhile products and deeply researched services, it is not so easy to copy and get away with it. Original creators will always have an edge over the copycats provided they are in tune with the markets. And these days intellectual property laws are strong in almost all nations.

Once we are through with the first iteration of creation, we can begin the most important process of pricing. At this point, we have the detailed market study and our own expenses till now to put a price tag on our product. We need to be abreast with all the latest pricing strategies discussed in management and entrepreneurship literature. Going through different case studies will help us either identify or creating a pricing model that will work best for us. Clearly the market should guide us more than our own expenses. The pricing should finally be based on how much a client is willing to pay. The expenses we have incurred in creating the product, including all the establishment and running cost of the company, tends to be the foundational factor. But we cannot depend on such a strategy that bases the price on our cost plus a profit percentage. That is a retail shop or trader mindset that will not help in expansion and scaling.

The value of a product or service is determined by the user and not the creator. So the estimate has to come from them. The same product and service or slightly tweaked versions might have immensely different value to customers operating in different market segment. All our knowledge gained from the hard work for market research is invaluable for us at this stage. It will help us arrive at ballpark figures for the various market segments that we are targeting.

Unless our creation is totally new and completely unheard of before, chances are that we have competitors who offer similar product of service. Their prices can also form a great guide for us. If we have managed a new system through which we can undercut their prices and still flourish, we can try it but without going too low. Going too low in the same market segment create a different impression about us. We will appear untrustworthy and low quality. So it is best to offer a slightly better price than the established competitor.

There are very successful companies that built exclusive brands by operating only in the high end market with select clients and keeping the price and quality extremely high. This is a decision we need to make. Are we keen on capturing the bigger market with a lower price or be high priced with fewer customers? Either route is fine. Our primary goal is to create a revenue stream that will sustain the company and allow it to grow at a pace that we desire.

This is a good juncture to bring some quantitative vigour to our market study. Three of the most important "numbers" that we should estimate and keep refining as we go along are: Total Addressable Market (TAM), LifeTime Value (LTV) and Cost of Acquisition (CoC). We may encounter these concepts under different names and abbreviations, but the essential idea is to give us a confident feel of the market. We will briefly touch upon on them here. There are plenty of online tools as well as good textbooks that explain in detail the significance and these methods to estimate these and other similar numbers.

Total Addressable Market is how much revenue we could make if we had 100% of the market share i.e. if all of our potential customers brought our product or service, how much money will we make? We can use market studies from our trusted consultants or our own surveys to estimate this number. This TAM number will help us in "planning big" as to the ultimate size of our company.

LifeTime Value and Cost of Acquisition are related to the customer. First one gives us how much revenue we can generate over time from each customer. Second one tells us what is the total amount we need to spend (marketing, sales and other expenses) to acquire each customer. These numbers are significant in evaluating the total valuation of the company. Valuation is, of course, critical when we seek funding.

In today's hyperconnected world, our competitors are everywhere. The upside is that we can also compete anywhere. So we should also consider entering geographically diverse market with a pricing strategy than can establish ourselves there. It will of course require support from a local team for marketing and sales, but those can also be factored in on the price. The Indian IT industry boomed because we could offer IT services at a much lower price to almost all the overseas market. We also watched some of the business disappear when other Asian countries become cheaper alternatives.

With the prototype or beta version ready and the business becoming a legal entity, we are once again ready to step out into the world for the next important C in the 7 Cs framework: Customisation!

7

The Sixth C: Customize

With our product prototype or service beta version ready, we embark on the customization step.

The word customise has the same root as the word customer. This is where we go back to the sample of ideal customers whom we had identified earlier. We return to them triumphantly with our creation which was based on their demand and our passionate effort. Now this may sound like a meeting made in heaven with everything going smoothly. Nothing could be farther from the truth.

First of all we need to identify the handful of customers in our beachhead market who we can approach for feedback about the prototype. They will be closest to what we had defined as the ideal customer. It is with their demands and inputs that we primarily designed the prototype. We must understand that the prototype becomes a product only after customisation ie input from the customer. We have to convince them also about it. What we are bringing to them is by no means a finished product ready to launch. We earnestly seek their feedback to finetune it.

They must understand at the outset itself that we are in no way attached to what we have created so far. If the customer senses our deep attachment and love for the prototype, sincere feedback will not be forthcoming. We are not approaching them for appreciation or encouragement. If we get those, that is great. But our objective is critical appraisal of what we have made and pointers to improvement.

The way we visualized and created the prototype might be totally different from what the customer had in mind in terms of look and feel, no matter how detailed the discussions we had. But make no mistake, it is only in the look and feel that the major chunk of this difference lies. If we had done our market study and customer interviews with all the seriousness and kept that in mind throughout the rest of the steps so far, then our product must satisfy nearly one hundred percent of the functionality demands.

However, it is human nature to judge things instantly in terms of look and feel. The customer upon "seeing" our prototype might be disappointed and even totally dejected. We must be prepared for this. This is the time where we need to patiently introduce to them all the functionalities. Make them look beyond the appearance of the product or the service. The appearance which is the color, texture, shape, size for physical products and the graphical user interface in terms of software, is easily changeable. If we focus our discussion only on that based on the customer's first impression, we will be walking down a dangerous path. To engage the customer in a discussion about the frills of the product before they get a chance to appreciate the functionality will not be productive.

So we need to be prepared for a long and patient first meeting. The time and venue of the meeting must be carefully chosen. As Daniel

Pink has amply illustrated in his hugely entertaining book "When," the timing of our meetings can by themselves influence the outcome. Similarly the setting of a meeting will color the cognitive bias of the participants.

Convince the customer that you are not attached to the look and feel of the prototype. Afterall, that is why it is called a prototype. Those things can easily be customized as per the exact demands of the client. Invite them to look under the hood. Dazzle them with the utility of the product, the functionalities of the software and capabilities of the service. Show them how is it exactly what they had demanded and much more. And convince them that this is just the first one in a series of meetings in which we will keep on tweaking the product till they are completely satisfied.

Collecting feedback is as important an art and science as our market research was. We need input from those in the customer team with different areas of expertise. Even if it is an individual, we have to weigh in the feedback he or she gives about various aspects of the prototype. Our questions should be well prepared in advance so that we can extract beneficial, actionable information from each conversation. We should have handy a quantifiable framework in which the responses can be sorted. The customer should not only suggest the changes but also tell us how important they consider that change to be for them to fall in love with the product. If they can rate the importance on a scale of say 1-5 or 1-10, it will help us in fixing the priority of making that change in our iterative customisation loops.

Our questions must be probing. A customer who wants no change in the prototype, unless they have visibly fall in love with the product with tremendous excitement, is simply dismissing us. In such cases, we must insist that they engage in answering our simple, specific questionnaire. We can leave it with them so that they can answer it at their convenience. Nevertheless, convince them how invaluable we consider their opinions and suggestions to be.

In some cases, it can happen that the customer has discovered a similar product while we were busy creating our prototype. It won't happen if we finish prototyping in a couple of months, but if our absence has been long and the product more sophisticated, we must take measures to prevent such a possibility. To avoid being blindsided in this scenario, we should have been intermittently in touch with the customer throughout the previous stages. Incremental stages of prototype need not be revealed to the customer, but a general update as an email once in a couple of weeks, will keep up the engagement. We can also use such communication to build up an interest in the product. Chances are high that any response we get during this stage will help improve the product.

Our internal review meetings at the end of each feedback session should produce itemized list of what changes we have to implement along with the priority. These should be executed under strict deadlines. The time frame for iterations and improvements towards final launch is crucial. With the customer interaction at this stage, there is a high chance that the cycle of improvement can repeat endlessly with new demands coming in all the time. So in the first meeting itself, we need to be very clear about our launch date. Till then, we should be prepared to work round the clock to incorporate all the top priorities of the customer. Fast turnaround time can in itself impress the customer to do further business with us. The speed with which we incorporate their demands and suggestions definitely reflects the future customer support that we will be providing them.

We need to get the customer also invested in the success of the product. Not in a monetary sense, but in the technical and emotional aspect. Once the product hits the wider market, there will be a lot of credit ascribed to our first set of "ideal customers." Though in many cases, these are just bragging rights, they do make a lot of business sense. It is part of the word of mouth marketing that is extremely important for a startup product. These customers will be present at our launch. They will be the first ones to recommend the product and write testimonials.

Just as it is said that imagining a future press release will help us get clarity in long term goal setting, we can imagine future testimonial that we expect from the customer as we go through these interactions. What aspects do we want them to like the most? How much should the product improve their business? These will help us also quantify and prioritise the iterative improvements that we undertake.

In our feedback interactions towards customisation, we have to ensure that the purchase decision maker of the customer company is involved substantially. Quite often it happens that the meetings get restricted to the engineering and technology teams. Design teams might get involved. But the decision makers might be on the sidelines. We must recognize that ultimately it is the actual buying decision makers who will make or break our product. All the recommendations, testimonials and encouragement don't mean much unless the customer spends money and buys our product.

To illustrate using a simple example. If we are designing a toy or an app for kids, all our important meetings in customisation will come from the little ones. But ultimately it is the parents and teachers who will decide about the purchase. So they must be kept in the loop respectfully.

A product becomes a perfect product only when the market calls it so. This means that we have to keep ourselves realistic in terms of the level of customer satisfaction we aim for from our sample of ideal clients. By having a disciplined and structured approach to the iterations coupled with strict deadlines of launch, we can get as close as possible to the perfect product.

Planning and Executing the Soft Launch

Despite the name, there is nothing soft about the soft launch. It is as serious and as important as a proper launch. We couch it in the softness simply to let it be known that adjustments are still possible based on immediate feedback before wider release. The launch is indeed a major event. It exposes our hard work of months and perhaps for years directly into the public eye for the first time.

Lot of planning need to go into the presentation of our product or service. The timing and date must be carefully chosen and prepared for much in advance. This is not yet another iteration. This is our announcement to the world that the product has arrived. Even though we choose to showcase it to a tiny cross section of the wider world. Where and to whom we soft launch the product to are the basic questions that need to be mulled over carefully and answered. Equally important is our expectations from the soft launch. What kind of response are we expecting from the market? What kind of feedback are we seeking? What is our plan of response to the event and for follow up?

This is the point where our company's marketing activities can come alive. With a brand new innovation, we have a lot of power with us to create and manage expectations. If we do it wisely during the soft launch phase, it can create a momentum that will keep the brand going for a long time. This is the starting point of our reputation building in a bigger circle. Soft launch is our first proper marketing exercise.

The event must be carefully planned with a curated guest list. The venue (it could be online as well) and hosting must reflect the quality that we have hoped to associate with the product. The audience will invariably end up associating the quality of the event with the quality of the product. So everything about the event matters. It is advisable to rope in professional event planners with experience to help us conduct the launch. This is not the beta testing phase. At the launch we are showcasing the "finished" product. It is good to outline the event carefully with the "peak-end" cognitive bias of human beings in mind.

We tend to judge any experience based on the peak effect it had on us and equally importantly how it ended. That is how the event will be filed away in our memory. This is why family vacations, no matter how incredible the location, leave us with unpleasant memory if they ended with a car breakdown or someone getting sick.

In case of our soft launch, we are relying on the audience to provide us maximum positive word of mouth. The best outcome would be the audience live tweeting or posting about our incredible little startup from the venue itself. But to give them something pleasantly memorable, we must be meticulous about how the momentum is build up during the event and how the experience ends for the guest.

8

The Seventh C: Compete

With our product/service ready and the soft launch successful, we sail into the final C in the framework. It is time to look at the competition anew. It is time to define our own sense of competitiveness.

There are hundreds of outstanding management books and brilliant articles available for our help in this stage. We must develop a habit of curated reading and application of the knowledge gained into our company's running. This is an essential habit to cultivate. Since high quality educational material is available elsewhere, this chapter offers only some basic pointers.

We had come across all the businesses offering products similar to ours in our concept and consulting stages. We produced innovation to differentiate ourselves from them as much as possible. Our beachhead market was carefully selected and ideal customer identified so that they are not within the cross hairs of any of our potential competitors. It could also be that we have such a drastically different product that we are establishing a market of our own, creating one as we go along.

Whatever be the scenario, once we are out in the public after the soft launch, we can rest assured that the competition has taken notice. Our presence might be expanding the market instead of cutting into their piece of the pie. But any innovation in their established area demands a response from all the existing players in the market. For some of them, not responding at all could also be a great response. Once in the market, we should not expect to be treated with soft gloves. The startup consideration and newbie treatment is reserved for incubators and supporting ecosystems. Market is the jungle. It is harsh in terms of its selection. Only the hardest working quick adapters with truly great quality can survive and thrive. We must compete in order to stay in the game and grow.

The first step in building our competitive muscle is assembling an A Team. This is the set of top notch people that we will hire to manage and run the operations of the company. We will need to establish, at least in a rudimentary sense, departments of finance, sales, HR, administration and so on. Each will have its own specialised team or those multitaskers who can play different roles suitably at different times. The first set of people we hire will invariably determine the quality of all further hires. So we must pick carefully and monitor carefully their performance till we are hundred percent sure that they are keepers. For a new company, it might be difficult to attract top talent, but we can attract the adventurous and the enthusiastic who can then grow with us.

Identifying Competition

With our customization process, we might have tweaked our product and service so much so that it starts affecting unexpected markets. Our idea and concept was developed in order to solve a particular problem faced by a sizeable population. But the tool we finally developed could have uses in far and wide areas that we did not anticipate. Remember Viagra! Nobody in the original biomedical research team that created the blue pill had any inkling of the sensational appeal of viagra in a totally different market segment.

With the soft launch and market expansion, we need to keep our eyes open for all the existing players in the markets who might even be remotely affected by our entry and positioning. We might be appealing to customers in a particular price band, but that doesn't mean a higher or lower price segment player feels safe. Neither should we. We should also pay close attention to international and other market players. It has become very easy in today's world to enter any market. So competition is truly worldwide.

We must keep ourselves abreast with the latest publications in our sector. Journals and magazines can give us a lot of food for thought. New startups and relevant latest university research must be closely studied. Whatever latest tech we can adopt into our own system must be immediately adapted.

Ethics and Quality

When we are in the game of gaining more market share, expanding the total market or invading a new market, there will be more than one possible route. Among the many routes, there will always be the tempting easy ones. These involve unethical steps, cutting corners and perhaps engaging in some corruption. If we are committed to building a world class sustainable enterprise, then we must not only be on guard against such tempting options but we must proactively resist them.

The easy route might fetch us some easy money. But it will always be only for the short term. Our aim must be to compete in terms of our innovation, quality and commitment to the customer. Those are the three firm legs which can guarantee profits in the long run. If the founding team is seen engaging in unethical practices, no matter how small, it affects the entire culture of the company. The firm adherence to transparency and quality should come from the very top. It must be reflected in every act of the business, whether it is scrutinized or not. This is the test that separates the real entrepreneurs from the short lived and one hit wonders.

Sustainability and growth in the long run is all about quality. When we study our competitors closely and thoroughly, it would appear that we can copy some of their aspects which will help us gain some more sales. But such imitation would quickly destroy the value of our brand. The same goes for trying to undercut a worthy competitor's prices just for competition's sake.

Using Competition to Grow

Competition makes our entrepreneurial journey exciting and perhaps arduous. Yet, it is the only way we can grow. Once we change our perspective and begin seeing competition as the motivation to aim higher and to do better, we can tap into immense energy provided by the competitive spirit. At this Compete stage, our company will be expanding in size. We must recruit the best possible people to manage the subsequent teams that we will set to take the company forward. The founders must never compromise on the direct recruitment that they do. Only with the best team of managers, we can hope for the best results. When the managers are in place, taking care of their responsibility, the founders can revisit our original vision.

We can set new targets and goals. Here, we can look at companies that are exemplary. We can aspire to match them in revenue, quality, brand recognition, employee satisfaction and so on. Let us use businesses that have made it big before us, to help us chart the path.

Once new goals are set, we must begin to compete with ourselves. We have already built the solid foundations for a company, now lets outdo ourselves in the growth targets that we have set for ourselves. Competing with our own apparent limitations is the best method to grow. Can we achieve more than we aimed for in less time and with higher quality?

Creating a healthy competitive culture for the company

As our team size grows, we will be assigning particular teams for particular tasks. There will be a product innovation team. This might be where the founders might be much inclined to stay. There will be sales teams that have been assigned different client accounts. There will be marketing teams targeting different markets. We need to design our company's culture with as much care as we put into designing our product. The culture forms the core strength. So it is important to develop a culture of healthy competition between the teams working in the company towards contributing to the overall growth.

Performance parameters can be fixed to analyse the team performance. These will obviously need continuous tweaking as both the company and the markets evolve. There must be regular appraisals and rewards for the better performing team. In these inhouse competitions, we can set the foundations for the ethical behavior and insist on transparency and quality that will percolate through out the company. Such practice will work much better in imbuing the spirit among the employees more than speeches and newsletters. Only when the vision and mission statements of the company take on a tangible form in the day to day company culture, we can be confident about building a strong enterprise.

Competing for Funds

We will not just be fighting it out in the market for potential customers. We will also be fighting with growing companies from all over the world for funding. Bankers, Venture Capitalists and Funding Agencies are always on the lookout for investment opportunities in promising companies. There are very few niche market investors. Most of the funding firms are open to good companies in any sector. That means we are competing with startups across the world.

We compete for their interest and money with our pitch. At this stage, we will be bringing in consultants who have do a valuation of our company as we prepare to part with some of the equity to gather fuel for expanding. The valuation process will help increase clarity of our vision.

Once again, we need to curate the list of available investors to pick the ones who will match our core values and whose presence can add more than just the monetary value. We need to read up and have more meetings with previously funded startups before we jump into bed with someone who can promise us big money.

If our revenue stream is smooth and cash flow comfortable, then we may not have to part with equity, but can take on debt based on our equation with the banks.

9

Cash: The Omnipresent C

I n this book, we have captured the major stages involved in the creation of an enterprise under seven headings. For ease of remembering, we have titled all of them with C words: Curate, Client, Concept, Consult, Create, Customize and Compete. There is however another C without which no enterprise can be born. Cash, as they say, is King! All entrepreneurs should develop a solid understanding of finances and respect the cash flow and bottom line at all stages. In this chapter, we will use the importance of cash or funds or financial management to also serve as a revision of the seven stages discussed so far.

Entrepreneurs can come from several different backgrounds. It can happen that someone in the founders team has an education in finance. But most often the founders are all either friends, colleagues who bonded while being in school or another company. And this need not be an MBA in finance or an accounting department. So one of the things the founders must religiously take it upon themselves from the beginning days itself is to have a solid understanding of finance and accounting.

We are not saying they should enroll in a part time MBA or accounting class. It doesn't matter if they grew up with a dread of mathematics. Accounting and finance is mostly restricted to addition and subtraction and occasional multiplication and division. Algebra, calculus and other mathematical fear inducing topics are never required. But if the entrepreneur shies away from understanding the mathematics behind the company's health, sooner or later they will, quite literally, pay the price.

In the curation stage, we should include a generous dose of financial publications in our reading. There are several excellent books available on the market. They avoid the intimidating jargon but provide excellent understanding of the foundations of finance and accounting. Spending time with such books will bring tremendous benefits in the long run. For those who are not avid readers (well, reading is one of the strong habits an entrepreneur must cultivate as we discussed in the curation chapter), there are two day or five day short courses and seminars delivered by experts that will get us upto speed. Online courses and youtube videos can also be used.

What have to learn the use of the basic numbers and the important financial statements related to a business. We should be able to understand the financial health of the company by studying these. Once we know how to use concepts like ROI, financial ratios, accruals, accumulations etc, we will be able to make much more informed decisions for our company. Understanding the balance sheet, income statement, cash flow etc provide us deep insights into performance of other companies as well. We need to figure out the "art of accounting" that exists behind the hard numbers. We are not trying to commit fraud or cook the books. We are aiming for financial intelligence. Its importance cannot be overstated. Because beyond the product and services, jobs and satisfied clients, not to mention improving the world, the single necessary and sufficient condition for the existence of a business is to make profit!

Developing such an understanding in the early stage itself, will give us one more vital dimension to use while doing the market analysis to pick our second C, Client. As we build the picture of our ideal client, looking for the decision makers and the cash controllers, being able to assess them using their financial statements will be a great plus. Most probably, our ideal target won't be individuals but companies, invariably if we are building B2B products/services. All registered companies will have their financial statements readily available. Even if they are not public, as in the case of listed companies, if we are able to talk to the leaders in their finance department, we can get a clear idea about how open they are, cash-wise, to trying out new products. The company's financial health will guide us in ballparking our product pricing. If our pitching and research conversations are peppered or sweetened (depending on your taste) with numbers that resonate with the client, the chances of success multiply.

Having a feel of the numbers is helpful particularly in our third C stage, Concept. While conceptualizing the company, money really matters. In the eyes of the wider economy, no matter what we create and how we operate, a business is ultimately a financial entity. Remember that this is the stage where we crystallize the idea of the company and the roadmap for the business. Our interactions with bankers, angel investors and venture capitalists will be based on this blueprint. All those folks are totally "money-minded" in a good way.

The most often heard complaint from the financiers about startup teams they meet, is their financial ignorance. The teams are unprepared about the numbers. They are so focused on the product development and lack any formal training in finance that it is a completely vague territory for them. While the founding team might have a sum they want to pitch to the investors, it might be pulled out of thin area without the kind of detailing that would interest and excite the investor.

All said and done, these interactions are fundamentally mere conversations. If we are able to speak the common language, use the familiar jargon with ease, it will instantly create a positive vibe. This is why it is important to get well versed in financial management terms. At least, we must be familiar if not well versed. Imagine how such meetings would go if the investor gets the feeling that the startup team is intimated or turned off by the numbers.

Our business concept must have a fully developed financial concept as well. Just like how we can describe the company in terms of what we do as product developers and marketers, we should be able to give a clear picture about the estimated cost, revenue and profit. Such planning will immensely benefit us as we consult with all the experts in the fourth stage C, Consult.

The experts we consult can give us more valuable insights if we present them our financial plan as well. With their experience, they can advise us if our estimates are way off or achievable. Such inputs will guide us in tweaking our business model into more realistic and reasonably ambitious milestones. The more financial numbers we estimate, the better our consultants can point out the potential pitfalls. We will definitely have to check the financial status of companies similar to us. This research will augment our market study.

Cash and finances become incredibly important in the Create stage. The quality of our product as well as the core team that we put together will depend on the kind of monetary planning and availability that we have. So many companies that start in bootstrap mode have had to compromise severely on the quality of their prototype. This tends to influence all further development in all departments. Be it the market segment, kind of investment, kind of employees and kind of final product, the company stumbles along a compromised path. On the other hand, startups that ensure that they have enough cash to create the best possible prototype put themselves in a different league altogether.

More than materials, the financial compromise gets severely reflected in the kind of people hired. Startups that have not thought through the cash requirement or financial health will undercut the quality of the initial hiring. Trying to keep the payroll expenses to a minimum, they will hire more interns or employees who don't demand a higher pay. We do not need to be flush with cash for hiring best of the best. If we have done our financial planning correctly, then any prospective high quality employee can see where the company is headed.

Detailed financial planning and execution will instill confidence in better people for coming onboard. They will understand that though the startup is currently in a bootstrap mode, accepting equity would be the wise thing to do. Only founders and leaders comfortable in talking numbers can exert such an influence. This is also true about the quality of consultants we may hire at this stage.

It is not just the prospective employees and consultants who are affected by our financial plan. Our own behavior is influenced by the level of comfort and expertise we establish in this department. It must be obvious by now that as entrepreneurs we cannot shy away from discussing money, deeply thinking about and actively planning around it. Too many startups have evaporated because of the habit of sweeping the financial concerns under the carpet in the pretext of product focus or market focus. By the time the founders realize that finance is their Achilles Heel, it is too late.

Financial management is an art and a skill. There may be people who have an inborn flair for numbers. Their brains might be able to process mathematical problems quickly. But we live in an era of supercomputers loaded on the chip of our smartphones. So mathematical processing ability is not a talent we require. Rest of financial acumen is a skill. And like all other skills, it can be learnt and expertise comes along with the time spent deliberately getting better at it. As entrepreneurs, we must commit to consciously learning more about finance and developing a genuine feel for the numbers. As time passes, we will be motivated more and more as we see the improvement it brings not only in the financial expertise but in better decision making that impacts the entire business.

Just as in the Create stage, budgetary concerns will determine how successfully we perform in the Customization stage. Our iterations and deadlines will be determined by how much we can invest in improvement of the product and how long we can sustain the company before the soft launch becomes unavoidable. For both these questions, the answer lies in our finance plan. Even the scale of our soft launch depends almost entirely on the kind of budget we can allot it. With social media and digital platforms, costs for creating a marketing campaign has come drastically down. But anyone guided solely by the idea of keeping cost down, will miss out on avenues that might be costlier but provide much better returns on the investment.

Return on Investment or ROI, is not just a financial concept to analyse stocks and other investment. It can be the best handy tool for any spending we plan to make. Which TV channel to choose or Social

Media Influencer to engage or which newspaper to advertise in should depend on the ROI they can provide rather than their absolute cost. But to be guided by ROI than absolute cost, we should have access to enough funds to consider all the possible options. If all we have is two lakhs to spend on the launch, then any option that costs double that is immediately off the table. With solid financial planning from the concept stage, we could already have allotted a budget for the soft launch in a scale that we think our product and firm deserves.

Needless to say, the Compete phase is fully dependent on the finances we can command. The kind of market penetration we can do will be based on how much we can spent. The marketing and sales execution will rely on funds available to them. The kind of competitors we can engage and clients we can canvas are determined by the kind of money we can allocate for such pursuits. This is why finance should be a major part of the planning exercise right from the beginning. It is as important as the planning for the market and the product. For those who are not educated in finance, it is easy to overlook. But we end up paying a tremendous price at the end for this error.

In the dreams of an entrepreneur, there will be visuals of successful product, beautiful launches, glorious market capture, satisfied clients, productive employees, limitless innovation and so on. But the fuel that powers all these visions is not just the entrepreneur's incredible energy but also the availability of funds. Money is the greatest friend or biggest foe an entrepreneur can have. Those who cultivate a respectful, confident, thorough and systematic relationship with finances will have a vastly different level of success. Once again, we must realize that it is a skill. So let us pledge to be lifelong students of financial management to ensure our success as entrepreneurs.

10

The Startup Habit

We have discussed the 7 C framework that can be used by budding entrepreneurs planning to embark on a new business. It can also be used by seasoned business creators as a structure for thinking through their future ventures. We discussed the common running thread of Cash as the important C through all the seven stages.

In my previous book, The Startup Habit, that I had coauthored with Dr. K C C Nair, known as the father of business incubation in Kerala, we had stated how starting up is a habit for entrepreneurs. The best entrepreneurs do not create just one company. They are never one hit wonders. For them, creating new ventures is a habit. I think it is appropriate to include as the final chapter in this book, the basic habits of an entrepreneur that constitute the Startup Habit.

Firstly, there is the excuse habit that plagues 95% of the population. People come up with wonderful ideas all the time. But the common mindset is to immediately think of excuses as to why those ideas cannot be pursued.Successful entrepreneurs tame this detrimental habit. We won't ignore it or wish it away. We will acknowledge its presence. We can use it wisely to filter out wasteful projects. The "excuse" habit seems to be the default of human brain which tries to avoid uncertainty at all costs. The mind abhors a vacuum. It wants to dwell in familiar grounds.

But any new venture comes with incredible uncertainty. Brand new products can only be created out of unexplored possibilities. An entrepreneur will recognize this excuse trajectory of the brain and tap into it. One of the greatest strengths for a successful business person is the ability to say No. If we say yes to all the projects that look promising, our energy and focus will be scattered. To say No to most of the projects that come our way, the excuse habit provides a wonderful starting point. Yet, we must be careful to ensure that it doesn't overwhelm our ideation and analysis potential. Ideation and Analysis are the two primary habits of entrepreneurs. Ideation and Analysis happen in the Curation stage of our framework. Entrepreneurs are always observing and listening. Like the legendary Richard Branson, it helps to carry a notebook or digital device around that can be used to note down potential opportunities we come across or ideas that strike us unexpectedly. All ideas must be treated with due consideration and respect. Whether to pursue them or not is dependent on the Analysis habit.

Analysis habit is the precursor to the Client Stage in our 7 C framework. When an idea is analysed, the entrepreneur thinks about its feasibility and market success. Such thinking can quickly help the entrepreneur separate an invention from an innovation. Remember how an innovation must contain commercialization potential. Otherwise it is a mere invention that might have technological, social or scientific benefit. But that never guarantees success in the marketplace. We can base our businesses only on ideas that can lead to revenue and profit generation.

Once the analysis tell us that the idea is worth pursuing, we move onto the execution habit. In a sense the 7 C framework provides a detailed step by step approach for this habit. Execution demands that we follow the stages carefully so that we create a healthy, sustainable and profitable business at the end of it.

The remaining four habits discussed under The Startup Habit are worth elaborating a bit more here.

The Resilience and Reflection Habits

Resilience is a habit of successful entrepreneurs. More commonly it is known as the ability to "bounce back." As mentioned earlier, entrepreneurship is all about dealing with uncertainty. We are creators of new products, we venture forth into unchartered markets, we deliver services unheard of till now. All along this wonderfully exciting path are potential pitfalls, setbacks, failures, let downs, disappointments and even heartbreaks. How we learn to deal with these determine our long term success!

Entrepreneurs embrace all feedback and failures as learning experience. We look at every step of the process as an experiment and not an examination. Thus we do not take negative treatment as a judgment. It might be a detrimental judgment but we can see that it is only context based. Our setback has nothing to do with our life as a whole, our character or the hard work we put in. Sometimes and may be most of the time, things don't work out as we had dreamt or planned. But whatever does happen is fodder for thought. This comes under the reflection habit.

In theory it is easy to say that we must overlook being judged. Social media allows anyone to comment on anything. It is prudent to ignore such snap, cheap judgment. It is also good advice not to judge ourselves. But these are very difficult to implement in real life. All of us feel low when things backfire, when doors are closed, when our attempts fail. One good habit that entrepreneurs can foster is to base the final self judgement only after accounting for the bouncing back as well.

Let us say that we were not granted a contract that we had hoped for. Our team had worked hard for several weeks. We had spent a good amount of resources. All the signs looks positive till the final announcement was made. Our hopes are dashed. We feel miserable. The team feels terrible. All this is natural. What happens the next day is what truly differentiate an entrepreneur. How much time do we choose to brood on our setback is entirely up to us. After giving ourselves time to process the failure, how quickly can be come back to our previous energy levels. How intensely can be convert it into a learning experience. How fast can we rally the team back again around the table to probe the experience for invaluable future lesson. Only after counting these further steps should we put a final judgment on how well we did with this experience. We must account for how well we bounced back and how deeply we reflected on each business lesson.

Consider a success scenario as well. We must certainly celebrate. Give ourselves a pat on the back. Once the partying is done, we need to sit and reflect on what worked out well. Unless we study our successes we won't know which elements to focus on and repeat. Our successes must become stepping stones for bigger future successes.

Reflection habit is also important for providing us the big picture. Once the business begins operating in full swing, we will be caught up in the day to day running. There will be fires to put out, crisis to handle, unending phone calls, hectic travel schedules, parties and conferences.

We need to find the time to be with ourselves regularly amidst all this. Solitude that has so beautifully been defined as the state of mind, free from inputs of other minds, is essential to our growth. The definition comes from the book, "Lead Yourself First" by Mike Erwin and Etheledge. As leader of our company, we need to lead ourselves first and for that we need to listen to ourselves. That can be done only in solitude through our Reflection Habit.

Growth and Ownership Habits

The two other habits that come under the Startup Habit are about Growth and Ownership. A business once created must continuously grow. This was briefly touched upon in the Compete stage of our 7 C framework. Without clear growth targets, the business will stagnate. The old adage of whatever is not growing is dying is particularly true for business. There will be plenty of scope for organic natural growth for the business especially if we have a brilliant product and clear market plan. But as leaders, we need to fix more aggressive targets so that our entire team can work on its full potential. If there is complacency or idled resources, lethargy will soon set it.

Growth can be chartered along several channels. We can fix targets in terms of revenue, market size, number of employees, profit, assets under management and so on. If we have developed excellent financial skills and feel for numbers, fixing SMART (Specific, Measurable, Attainable, Relevant and Timely) targets will be much more effective. When we can ensure that our goals/targets are SMART in nature, pursuing them will be more systematic.

Among the various channels, there will be some that are more attuned to our inner nature. An entrepreneur must pick on these early on itself. Our greatest satisfaction might come from growth in a particular area. For example, it might be the bottom line profit for some, employee satisfaction for others or market penetration for some others. We must make sure that this bias is aligned with the overall growth of the company. It must not skew our priority and make this growth possible at the expense of limiting expansion in others.

Like the need for leading ourselves first, the growth of the company must be a reflection of our own deep desire for continuous personal growth. Building our personality, skills and strengths is a never ending process. An entrepreneur must have clear plans and processes for this as well. It is a habit that will lay the foundation for all the other habits. The greatest joy of being an entrepreneur is that we are not fixed into a particular employment position based on our qualification. And we get the added satisfaction of helping the position of everyone who works for our enterprise.

Ensuring the growth of everyone involved with our business, including the suppliers, contractors, consultants and clients, we can ensure our own personal, professional and profitable growth.

The ownership habit deserves special attention. As students or as employees, we receive precious little preparation for running our own companies. We might have been exemplary students. We might have been responsible employees. But owning our own business is different from being responsible. Of course, we might be responsible for a particular role in the company, but ownership is something that defines our relationship with the company in its entirety.

The best analogy to explain the relationship is that of parenting. Really good parenting that is. The parents are totally responsible for the child. This total responsibility also gives them total freedom to make decisions. We are talking about a baby or very small child here, so leave aside the implications of the child's rights for a while.If the child falls sick, the parents will of course take her to the best available doctor. The doctor might be a very responsible person. He can diagnose and tell the parents exactly what the problem with the child is. But as far as the parents are concerned, such responses mean nothing. Their only concern is making the child better, restoring back to health. Similarly our managers, employees, consultants and advisors might be able to tell us very responsibly what is wrong with our company or what needs to be done, but it is upto us to make sure that action is taken for the best course of growth.

This kind of ownership we need to have towards our own life. Our life can have innumerable unexpected events. Some may be great, many may be unfortunate. But if we proceed along without any plans and let the events guide us, we will never reach our full potential. As Jim Rohn says we will land somewhere in the future for sure if we let the tides take us, but isn't it better to land somewhere we planned to be or at least near abouts. Such ownership of life must inspire us to take ownership of our family and the greater society.

Entrepreneurship cannot exists separate from the society. Wealth creation demands the upliftment of as many as possible, may be through employment directly or indirectly or through products and services that improve lives, directly or indirectly. When we let such concern for as many as possible guide our decisions, they become easier and more meaningful.

World Bank report of 2019 estimates that the world needs 600 million jobs in the next 15 years to absorb the youth entering the workforce and maintain the current quality of life. A whopping majority of this will be needed in the developing countries and will have to come from the private sector. The world depends on more entrepreneurs who can create new ventures to provide more jobs. The importance of the task ahead of us cannot be overstated.

Once we launch our first venture, working through the 7 Cs of the framework diligently, we will be on our way to embracing the startup habit. With each company entering a steady growth pattern, we will have time to embark on new ventures armed with greater experience and expertise.

Here's to all the future ventures, personal and professional across the seas!